Mary *and* Martha

a novel

OTHER BOOKS AND AUDIOBOOKS
BY H.B. MOORE
Out of Jerusalem: Of Goodly Parents
Out of Jerusalem: A Light in the Wilderness
Out of Jerusalem: Towards the Promised Land
Out of Jerusalem: Land of Inheritance
Abinadi
Alma
Alma the Younger
Ammon
Daughters of Jared
Esther the Queen
The Moses Chronicles: Bondage
The Moses Chronicles: Deliverance
The Moses Chronicles: Exodus
Ruth
Anna the Prophetess
Deborah: Prophetess of God

OTHER BOOKS BY
HEATHER B. MOORE
Women of the Book of Mormon: Insights & Inspirations
Christ's Gifts to Women
Divinity of Women: Inspiration and Insights from Women of the Scriptures
Athena
Ruby's Secret
Tying the Knot

MARY *and* MARTHA

a novel

H.B. Moore

Covenant.

Covenant Communications, Inc.

Cover image *Mary and Martha* by Robert A. Boyd; for more information go to RobertABoyd.com

Cover design copyright © 2020 by Covenant Communications, Inc.

Published by Covenant Communications, Inc.
American Fork, Utah

Printed in the United States of America
First Printing: November 2020

10 9 8 7 6 5 4 3 2

978-1-52441-442-9

In loving memory of Kris Belcher.
You are missed.

CHARACTER CHART

*Indicates fictitious names

Martha
Mary
Lazarus
Mary Magdalene
Mary: mother of James
Andrew
Simon Peter
Judas Iscariot
Thomas
Simon: the leper
*Leah: wife of Lazarus
*Rhode: son of Lazarus
*Nathaniel: son of Lazarus
*Naomi: daughter of Lazarus
*Asher: son of Lazarus

*Josiah: herb seller
*Zachary: widower
*Claudia: Zachary's daughter
*Horeb: man in Galilee
*Yosef: first husband of Martha
*Isaac: Mary's betrothed
*Delilah: Isaac's mother
*Sarah: blind woman in Galilee
*David: landowner
*Eunice: neighbor, David's wife
*Joel: neighbor
*Phebe: neighbor
*Tamara: neighbor
*Elder Gideon: synagogue instructor
*Benjamin: village man

CHAPTER ONE
Martha

MARTHA KNELT ON THE PATCH of stubby grass poking through the stony ground of her late husband's burial place. Yosef had been gone three years now, but her grief had yet to ebb. A gust of winter wind tugged at her mantle, and she grasped it tightly beneath her chin. She rarely came to the burial ground so late in the day, but this past week had been extra busy with preparations for the betrothal celebration for her younger sister, Mary.

Closing her eyes for a moment against a sky splashed gold and violet with the setting sun, Martha refocused on her memories of Yosef. They'd been married less than a year, and no children had resulted from their union. Yosef had been a kind, fair man who owned the olive grove next to her family's. Yosef and Martha's brother, Lazarus, had made many journeys together to Galilee to trade and sell olive oil.

It was during one of his journeys that Yosef had been waylaid by bandits on the road through the Jordan Valley.

Martha would never forget the day her brother, Lazarus, had delivered the news to her. Even now, at the memory, her eyes burned with too-familiar tears.

"Papa, is that woman sad too?"

Martha heard the small voice before she saw a man with a young girl coming up the slope that rose from the village. Martha opened her eyes but remained kneeling on the winter grass, her hands clutching her mantle.

The man murmured something Martha couldn't hear.

"Can we speak to her?" the young girl asked, her voice clear and carrying on the wind like an errant feather.

The man's next reply was audible but low. "We don't want to interrupt her contemplation."

"What is *contemplation*?" the girl asked.

Martha almost smiled. The question was a fair one for a child so young. Even at a quick glance, Martha guessed the child to be six or seven.

The man's patient sigh was scattered by the wind, and Martha wondered what had brought this man and his daughter to the burial site.

"*Contemplation* means that someone is remembering their loved ones," the man continued.

"Like Mother is our loved one?"

The child's forlorn voice wedged itself into one of the cracks of Martha's heart, and her attention again strayed to the man and child.

The father held his daughter's hand as they stood over a tomb marker, the wind making brisk work against their clothing. Curiosity ebbed through Martha as she tried to identify the man. His dark curls reached his shoulders, and his beard was cut short. He was tall, lean, and his face was tanned from the outdoors, although they were in the middle of the cold season.

His daughter's long hair was plaited over her shoulder, and her clothing hung loose, as if it had been fashioned from a much larger garment.

Ah, now Martha recognized the pair. She'd never met them formally because they lived on the outskirts of Bethany. Zachary was the man's name, and he was a shepherd who'd relocated from Jerusalem after a land dispute with his twin brother. The story that had circulated throughout the village was that Zachary had given up his land inheritance in exchange for two-thirds of the family flocks.

She wasn't sure what his daughter's name was, but Martha remembered the funeral of his wife only weeks before. She'd died delivering an infant son, and the babe had died as well.

So much death, the swirling wind seemed to whisper. *So much tragedy. So much despair.*

Martha's heart felt like it was being crushed between two stones. She didn't want to remember her own losses right now. There was no time anyway. This short escape from her chores was all she could afford, and then she had to return and grind enough barley for the extra bread she'd make for the betrothal ceremony guests.

Martha missed Yosef with a renewed pang, but as she looked at the father and daughter, she realized she'd been fortunate to have both her parents throughout her childhood, as well as her two siblings, Lazarus and Mary.

And Yosef's remains were deep in the tomb beneath the stone slab she knelt next to. His family tomb, like many of the family tombs on this rocky hillside above her village of Bethany, held generations of memories and lives lost too soon. At least he'd been buried in the town of his birth.

Before Martha could lower her eyes, Zachary looked up. In the instant before the vagabond shepherd nodded in acknowledgment, she saw the depth of his grief. Martha recognized that grief right away because it had been her constant companion these past three years.

The little girl's round, dark eyes reminded Martha of a young doe. The child waved, hope in her expression, and Martha felt that hope reach across the stony ground separating them.

Martha released her mantle to wave back.

"She waved at me, Papa," the little girl whispered in a voice that wasn't really a whisper.

Martha felt she should go. Although she was a widow, it would not be proper to converse alone with a single man, even if he was with his young daughter.

Rising to her feet, Martha once again grasped her mantle beneath her chin. Then she mouthed a silent prayer to Adonai—over her siblings, her niece and nephews, and especially Lazarus in his travels. She finished with prayers for endurance, continued health, and patience.

Before twilight could fully descend and darkness take over the land, Martha hurried down the hillside and through the lanes of Bethany until she reached her home. Well, Lazarus's home now. When Yosef died, Martha had moved back to her parents' home since she couldn't very well claim any of Yosef's inheritance without any sons. She'd occupied the third level of her parents' home with Mary, while Lazarus's family had resided on the second level. After her father's death, Lazarus had moved his family down to the main level of the house, and Mary had taken over the second level.

His wife, Leah, was carrying their fourth child, to be born in the spring, so Martha and Mary spent more time in the cooking room than ever. At least Martha did. Mary had been busy working on a new mantle, and the embroidery was turning out beautifully.

Entering the courtyard of her home, Martha nearly tripped over a small goat. The creature bleated, and she patted its head. "How did you get out of your pen? And where's your mama?" she asked, nudging the goat through the courtyard. "Come on."

She guided the goat around the side of the house and to the rear courtyard, where the goat and chicken pens were. She stopped in her tracks at the sight of disarray. One of the pens was open, and the mother goat and three other kids were roaming the yard.

"Rhode! Nathaniel! Come help me!" she called, hoping her voice would carry into the house, then she remembered they were at the synagogue tonight.

"What is going on?" Leah's voice cut through the bleating.

Martha turned to see her sister-in-law standing framed in the back entrance. Leah's normally round, smiling face was creased in concern. "Oh goodness."

Martha effectively corralled the mother goat into the pen, then she latched the gate shut. Next, she scooped up one of the kids, lifted it over the gate, and set it inside with its mother. The other two kids scattered, enjoying their new freedom.

"There's one." Leah pointed toward the corner of the house.

Martha took off after it. The little goat was fast, though, and sensed it was being chased. But Martha snagged the kid before it could escape to the front courtyard. When she arrived in the back courtyard again, Leah was smiling.

"I'm glad this amuses you," Martha teased.

"I'm sorry." Leah's smile only widened. "I am impressed with how fast you move."

Martha set the second kid over the gate, then turned, scanning the nearly dark yard.

"It went under the wagon." Leah's voice bordered on a laugh.

"Wonderful." Martha huffed, then moved to the wagon and peered under it. It was too black to see anything. "Come here." She snapped her fingers, but no goat appeared.

"All right then," Martha mumbled. She knelt and crawled under the wagon. It was pushed against the wall of the stable, so there was no way it could escape the other side.

Two eyes watched Martha as she inched forward, scraping her hand in the process. She waited for the stinging to subside, then moved more. The little goat bleated as she edged closer.

"Come on," Martha soothed, then grasped the goat by the scruff of its neck. It was a bit trickier to crawl back out with the animal, but soon she emerged, filthy but successful.

Leah had stepped into the yard, her hands set on her hips. "Nicely done, sister."

They weren't sisters by blood, but Leah called both Martha and Mary *sister*.

"Thank you," Martha said. "Rhode and Nathaniel can be the ones to brush down my clothing when they return from the synagogue."

"I agree," Leah said, though her tone was affectionate. "Hang your outer clothing by the door, and I'll have them do it before they eat."

Leah was one of those women who never became frazzled with her children's antics. Rhode was thirteen and Nathaniel eleven. Little Naomi was four. Perhaps because there were several years between Nathaniel and her next child, Leah enjoyed every stage of childhood to its fullness. And now, her fourth child should arrive in a few months.

With all the goats back in their pen, Martha followed Leah into the house. Martha slipped off her outer robe and hung it on a peg, then she washed in the basin kept near the door. "What can I help with?"

"I can finish the meal preparations," Leah said. "You continue with whatever you're working on for the banquet."

"Are you sure?" Martha scanned the meal in progress.

"I am sure." Leah moved to the fireplace, where she had a bubbling stew over the fire. On the wood table, she'd been preparing vegetables. Honey cakes already sat cooling on a length of cloth.

"All right. I'll call down Mary, and she can help wherever is needed." Martha headed up the narrow flight of stone stairs. Once Leah's fourth child was born, Lazarus was thinking about moving the two boys to the second level, which meant that Mary would want to move upstairs with Martha. It would be fine. In less than a year, Mary would wed and move into her new home with her new in-laws.

"Mary?" Martha called as she climbed the stairs. Her right hand stung a little from scraping it on the ground when she'd crawled under the wagon.

No answer came from her sister, but that didn't necessarily mean much. Her sister had been spending her time writing and reading when she wasn't working on her embroidery. And often, Mary, an unusual girl who'd learned to read and write, would become caught up in whatever text she was deciphering and forget the hum of life around her.

Martha headed into the first bedchamber on the second floor. An oil lamp burned low, but there was no Mary. Her platform bed was unmade, as if it were early morning instead of evening. The bed was made up of a padded mat that sat atop a series of ropes, crisscrossed both side to side and end to end.

A wooden table was covered with scrolls of papyrus borrowed from Lazarus.

Then Martha caught sight of the movement of a blowing curtain against a single window in the room. Her breath caught when she saw a length of cloth tied to a hook at the base of the window. What was Mary up to now?

Martha crossed to the window and looked at the courtyard below. The cloth extended about halfway down the outside of the house. Right away, Martha knew her sister had escaped the house through her bedchamber window. Where was her sister, and why had she left?

CHAPTER TWO
Lazarus

GALILEE WAS BEAUTIFUL IN WINTER despite the dormant flowers, dull-colored grasses, and crisp morning air. Lazarus decided he loved all faces of the land—when she was at her most glorious or when she was at her most subdued. This morning would be his last day at the market before he made his way back home to Bethany, a three-day trek if there were no incidences or the Sabbath to interfere.

Lazarus missed his family, and he'd been worried about leaving his wife, Leah, when she was so close to delivery. But the winter trading in Galilee was the most profitable because olive oil reserves began to run low in most households.

The sounds of animals, mostly donkeys and cattle making it known that they were ready for sustenance, pulled Lazarus from his mat upon the hard floor of the small inn he'd paid to stay in. He never traveled extravagantly, even though he had the means to do so. With a budding household of soon-to-be four children, plus both of his sisters dependent upon him, Lazarus didn't like to spend money on unnecessary luxuries when the money could be put to better use.

Lazarus stretched his back. It ached as usual, a side effect of traveling from home. In another year, Lazarus would include Rhode in some of his trading journeys, but for now, the boy was better off focusing on his learning. So Lazarus traveled alone. It hadn't always been that way.

Martha's husband, Yosef, had been his traveling partner, even before the marriage. Although they were technically in competition with each other, Yosef had always been fair-minded. Selling olives and olive oils to the northern towns and villages brought in a healthy profit, and there was room for two olive growers from Bethany.

"You stubborn beast." A deep voice cut into the morning stillness.

The sound came from outside somewhere, and Lazarus peered out his tiny window. In the middle of the courtyard, which was dimly illuminated by approaching dawn, a young man was trying to shove his donkey into motion. But the effort was weak at best since the man's left foot was severely deformed. He had to put most of his weight on his right foot, which gave him very little leverage against a full-grown donkey.

The donkey was intent on a patch of grass that had somehow survived all the trodding footsteps, and no wonder, for the animal's ribs were prominent. The donkey looked next to starving.

"Move!" the man yelled.

Lazarus knew it was only a matter of time before the occupants of the surrounding inn would awaken, and none would be pleased.

"Can I help you?" Lazarus called down to the young man.

He raised his chin with a jerk, his dark eyes wide with surprise at the intrusion.

"I've dealt with an animal or two in my time," Lazarus added.

The man's expression of frustration didn't dissipate. "I've nothing to pay you."

"I don't need payment," Lazarus said. "I'll be out in a moment." He slipped on his outer robe, strapped on his sandals, then grabbed a couple of vegetables from the food basket in his bedchamber. Soon he hurried into the courtyard.

The young man was still there, and so was the donkey, who hadn't budged at all.

"I'm Lazarus," he said, nodding at the young man. He was younger than Lazarus had thought at first, and he guessed the lad to be in his early twenties.

"I'm Horeb," the young man said. He wiped at the perspiration on his brow. Aside from the gauntness of his cheeks, he was a fine-looking fellow. The beginnings of a beard showed up as dark scruff on his jaw. It was plain he was barely above the status of a beggar and his donkey was not far off from starvation.

"Where are you headed to before the sun rises?" Lazarus asked.

"I seek the man they call Jesus," Horeb said. "Jesus of Nazareth. They say he is in Galilee right now, and I intend to find him."

Lazarus frowned. During his temple trips to Jerusalem, he'd heard of Jesus, but never in favorable terms. What were Horeb's intentions? "It's quite early. Do you plan to wake Jesus out of slumber by knocking on his door?"

Horeb's brow pinched. "He's a wanderer, so he has no door. But He can heal my foot if only I can find Him in time."

"Oh, so this man is a physician?" Lazarus didn't remember the title applied to what he'd heard about Jesus. He didn't want to discourage this young man, but physicians were expensive.

"No," Horeb said. "He's a healer who possesses the power of Adonai."

Something warm prickled the back of Lazarus's neck. "What do you mean?"

"Jesus has healed the blind, the dumb, the lame, and the maimed." Horeb's voice rose with fervency. "And He can heal my foot if only I can get this donkey to move."

This young man's conviction was astounding. Surely Lazarus would have heard of these deeds if they'd been true. A maimed foot healed with some unseen power would not go unnoticed by the Pharisees, who paid attention to any unusual goings-on.

Horeb's voice fell to a pleading. "Please, if there is any way you can get my donkey to move, I would be grateful until the end of my days."

If anything, Lazarus was intrigued. He pulled one of the vegetables out of his robe pocket, and the donkey immediately lifted its head. Lazarus offered the vegetable to the animal, who ate it readily. Then he held the next vegetable a few paces away. The donkey moved forward, and Lazarus moved backward, drawing the animal out of the courtyard. At the edge of the courtyard, he fed the donkey its reward.

"Thank you, good man," Horeb said. He hobbled after the donkey, then managed to climb atop the animal with clearly practiced skill.

Lazarus handed the final vegetable to the young man, and the donkey continued walking with Horeb, who encouraged it to move faster and faster. Though the donkey never picked up pace, it didn't stop either.

Lazarus stood for a moment, watching the pair as they traveled in the direction of Galilee, the opposite direction Lazarus had come the day before. The young man's thin shoulders bounced up and down with the movement of the donkey, and Lazarus wondered at the determination he'd seen in Horeb's eyes. Lazarus hoped the young man would be healed or at the very least find some relief from his challenges. But whether that healing or relief came from the man from Nazareth was another matter altogether.

Glancing at the eastern horizon where the sun's rays had begun their slow crawl toward the valley, Lazarus felt his heart soar. In three days, he would be home, scooping little Naomi into his arms, pulling his wife into a soft embrace, and catching up with his sons and on the week they'd all spent without him.

Lazarus had no doubt his sisters, Martha and Mary, had entered the final stages of preparations for Mary's betrothal banquet. She would marry Isaac in a few months' time, so the betrothal was the next step toward that event.

And now, it was time to prepare for his journey. He had his own donkeys to feed and prepare. Lazarus glanced at the retreating figure of Horeb and his donkey, then turned toward the inn, making it only a few paces before he heard a cry coming from the road.

He spun around to see Horeb on the ground and, next to him, the donkey sprawled in the dirt. They hadn't gotten very far, and Lazarus ran toward the pair. "What happened?" he called as he drew near. "Did the donkey trip?"

But Horeb wasn't answering; he wasn't even looking at Lazarus. Horeb knelt over the donkey's inert body and began to plead with an unseen person about his donkey.

It took only a moment for Lazarus to realize Horeb was praying—out loud with wild gestures. Lazarus frowned, not sure if he should reprimand the man for his highly unusual prayer style, but then he heard the words.

"O Lord, my God, breathe life into this beast so that he might carry me to Galilee. Save your vengeance for another day. Tomorrow I will take any punishment."

Lazarus moved around to the other side of the donkey and, with a sinking heart, realized the beast was worse off than he'd first thought; the donkey was nearly starved, and it seemed he'd given up.

"Thou has the power to raise the dead and heal the sick, O Lord," Horeb continued, tilting his face to the heavens. "What is a small creature in your eyes? This will only take a moment of your time. Please, O Lord, I beg of you—"

"Horeb," Lazarus cut in, grasping the man's shoulders. "Your donkey is weak and starving. No amount of prayer is going to restore its health."

It was as if Horeb hadn't heard a word from Lazarus, as if he didn't even exist. "O Lord, my God, hear my prayers." He raised his hands toward the sky. "Hear the pleadings of my heart. I have lived with much suffering my entire life, and now, when I am so close to receiving deliverance, my donkey—"

"Horeb," Lazarus cut in again. He grasped one of the man's hands and tugged it downward. Horeb was surprisingly strong for such a thin man. "The donkey isn't going anywhere unless he has days of food and rest. I am sorry."

Horeb's gaze shifted to Lazarus, then he lowered his arms voluntarily. "If I cannot reach Jesus, I will be lame the rest of my life," he whispered. "Don't you see? This donkey was my last hope, and now he cannot take another step. My parents are dead. This donkey is all I own, and now he, too, cannot go on."

Horeb buried his face in his hands.

He wasn't crying or wailing, but Lazarus could feel every bit of the young man's despair. The morning air warmed a fraction as the sun's rays finally reached the valley road. The winter morning was quiet now, but soon, travelers would begin to appear. Lazarus doubted a random stranger would extend a helping hand to this grieving young man. A man with nothing to offer, with no money to pay, a man who could not even walk on his own two feet.

Lazarus placed a hand on the donkey's neck. The beast was still breathing, but he was suffering. With greater care, was there hope for the animal?

"Horeb, my friend," Lazarus said at last. "I will ask the innkeeper to care for the donkey. He needs nourishment and rest. While the donkey is recovering, I will take you to Galilee. We will find this man you speak of."

Horeb didn't move for a moment, then, slowly, he lifted his dark head. Silent tears streaked his cheeks, but his face was aglow with wonder. "But you said you are due in your village."

"I am," Lazarus said simply. "My family will understand when they learn I needed to help a friend."

Horeb wiped at new tears on his face with his grimy fingers. "You are a good and generous man, but I cannot pay you. And I cannot pay the innkeeper for his care."

Lazarus couldn't help the laugh that escaped him despite the situation. "I know, Horeb. I am not asking for money." He rose to his feet and extended his hand.

Horeb rubbed a sleeve over his eyes, then looked up at Lazarus with incredulousness in his expression. He placed a hand in Lazarus's, and Lazarus pulled him to his feet.

"I don't know how to thank you," Horeb said.

"Someday, when you are in a position to help another, do it in my honor."

Horeb swallowed and nodded. He took a staggered step forward, and Lazarus put a hand on his shoulder. "Wait here," Lazarus said, not wanting the man to have to hobble all the way back to the inn "I'll speak to the innkeeper, then return shortly with my cart, and we'll go find your Jesus."

The process of collecting his things, paying the innkeeper for the room and offering extra money for the care of the donkey, loading the cart, and preparing his own two donkeys took longer than expected. But Horeb wasn't going anywhere; he was sitting on the side of the road only paces away from the exhausted donkey when Lazarus arrived to collect him.

Horeb scrambled to his feet as Lazarus approached.

"I thought you'd changed your mind," Horeb said.

"Not at all," Lazarus said, slowing the cart so that Horeb could climb up beside him. "It turns out that more than just your donkey was stubborn this morning."

Lazarus followed Horeb's gaze; the innkeeper was bringing a cart and a couple of men to transport the donkey back to the stables.

"When we return, your donkey will have recovered."

Horeb blinked rapidly, then nodded. "I will pray that to be the case."

After seeing Horeb settled into the cart, Lazarus climbed in too. He clicked his tongue, and the donkeys set off. They passed the winter landscape, mostly barren this time of year. It was no wonder Horeb's donkey was in such poor shape. The winter had stripped the hills of most grasses and flowers, and if Horeb had no money for grain, the poor beast was surely overworked.

As the donkeys and cart descended into the valley, the Sea of Galilee spread before them, blue and gold in the early morning light.

Horeb told of his youth, which was not so long ago. He hadn't known his father, and his mother served in a merchant's household. Horeb had been born with his lame foot, but from the moment Horeb was able to speak, he was put to work in the stables behind the master's estate. He cared for the cattle, donkeys, and mules.

When his mother died two years before, the master had given him a donkey and sent him on his way. Horeb had wandered ever since, working for whomever would pay him, but it seemed one bad fortune followed another. He'd been called lazy, accused of theft, even told he was dimwitted when he hadn't grasped the concept of measurements for a grain trader.

"If my foot can be healed, then I will become a man of fortune," Horeb told Lazarus.

It was a bold statement, both in the belief of healing and going from a near beggar to a wealthy man.

Lazarus glanced at the young man and the determined set of his jaw. "If Jesus has no house in Galilee, where will we find Him?"

"Everyone will know," Horeb said with conviction. "We've but to ask."

So they continued on as the rising sun dispelled the sharpness of the cool air. They passed a few huts, but all seemed quiet in the outskirts. Then Horeb said, "There! Look!"

Lazarus looked to where Horeb was pointing. In a field up ahead, a group of people were huddled close to a fire as they warmed meat upon a spit over it. "Jesus is among them?"

"I don't know," Horeb said, his words rapid with excitement. "If not, they might be followers."

Lazarus slowed his cart as they reached the edge of the field. Horeb hopped out of the cart, then limped over to the group of people. Lazarus couldn't hear the conversation, but when Horeb turned and walked back to the cart, his expression was elated. With him, he guided an elderly woman who appeared to be blind. She took careful steps along the stony ground, and with Horeb's lame foot, the pair made slow progress.

Once they reached the cart, Horeb said, "This is Sarah. Do you think she can ride in the cart instead of me? I will let her take my place."

Lazarus couldn't turn the request down. "Of course. Where are we taking her?"

Sarah's wrinkled face broke into an almost toothless grin. "To Jesus. They say He is camping not far from here. We need to travel east."

"Yes," Horeb said. "There are already hundreds of people traveling to hear from Him, so we must hurry."

Lazarus's brows pulled together. "Hundreds?"

"There will soon be thousands once His location is known." Horeb's brown eyes were warm with excitement. "Can we leave now and let Sarah ride?"

"You may both ride," Lazarus said. "These donkeys are spoiled with no cargo, and they need to keep up their strength."

Horeb chuckled. "I will not turn down the offer, then."

Lazarus helped Sarah into the cart and saw that she was settled. Horeb hoisted himself in as well, then they were on their way again, feeling every rock under the wheels.

Horeb chattered to the woman, telling her how he'd been rescued by Lazarus when he was at his deepest despair. The young man certainly had the gift of storytelling because Lazarus found himself captivated by the tale about himself.

Lazarus slowed the donkeys' pace as they rounded a bend onto a smaller road. Beyond the bend, a hill rose, one littered with people. Carts and donkeys blocked Lazarus from getting closer to the hillside. He couldn't even pass.

"What's going on?"

"All of these people are seeking healing from Jesus, just as I am," Horeb said, his tone reverent.

Lazarus pulled the cart to a stop and scanned the rising slope full of people. Some were milling about, others were standing in small groups, and many were sitting on bedrolls, as if waiting for instruction. This was no ordinary gathering but one filled with some people using canes, some with their eyes bound with cloth, others obviously maimed in some way.

Which man was the one they called Jesus?

"Jesus is here," Sarah said. "I can feel Him."

Her words sent a warm shiver along Lazarus's arms. Sarah was blind, but that didn't seem to slow down her other senses.

"Let's go," Horeb said. "It will take us awhile to climb that slope."

"How steep is it?" Sarah asked, already shifting her weight to the back of the cart.

"Not too steep," Horeb assured the woman.

Lazarus marveled at the pair. He could only hope they wouldn't be disappointed for their efforts. He moved to the back of the cart, and together they helped Sarah down.

"Hold on to my arm," Horeb said, "as tight as you want."

Sarah clung to Horeb's arm with both hands. Surely he wasn't planning on climbing that hill with both his lame foot and a blind woman hanging on for support?

Horeb turned to Lazarus. "Thank you for everything," he said in a voice thick with emotion. "If it wasn't for you, I would not be here. I hope our paths cross again someday, my friend."

Lazarus's own throat tugged tight. He eyed the hill, then looked at the pair before him. "I will take you up the hill."

Horeb's dark brows pinched. "It's too steep for the cart, and the donkeys could get injured if they lose their footing."

Lazarus was not a young man, but he was sturdy, and he'd carried and loaded plenty of baskets weighted with olives over the years. And Horeb was tall but thin and likely weighed about as much as Rhode. "I'll take you up on my back, then return for Sarah."

"I can walk," Sarah said. "I'll need to hold on to you, but I can walk."

Horeb scratched at the scruff on his jaw. "You've already been so generous, Lazarus. I don't want to keep borrowing your hospitality."

Lazarus turned and crouched before Horeb. "On my back."

Horeb hesitated, then obliged, and Lazarus gripped the end of the cart to keep his balance while he adjusted to the new weight on his back and straightened.

"Sarah?"

She grasped his upper arm. "Ready."

They might have made a spectacle if the gathering on the hillside wasn't already its own collection of people with crippled limbs, withered hands, and distressed countenances.

Lazarus scanned the crowd as he trudged up the hill. Most were moving in the same direction, though some had taken a break from the climb and were sitting on the sloped ground. Horeb's weight increased the higher Lazarus climbed, but it couldn't be much farther now, could it?

"Do you recognize Him yet?" Lazarus puffed out.

"I have never seen Him," Horeb said.

"Neither have I," Sarah said.

Horeb laughed at Sarah's reply. And despite the fact that Lazarus was perspiring and breathing hard, he smiled.

"So what are we looking for, then?" Lazarus asked. Surely this Jesus fellow wouldn't be at the very top of the hill, would He?

But then Lazarus saw Him—at least a man who had to be Him because He stood in the midst of others, holding the withered hands of a man whose beseeching eyes held a hope similar to that in Horeb's expression.

Horeb spotted him at the same time. "It's Jesus," he whispered.

Lazarus continued toward Jesus, curious about what He was saying to the man with withered hands. Lazarus caught the words, which sounded like a prayer or a blessing of healing. Before Lazarus could get any closer, another man in an indigo robe intercepted his path and pointed. "You must take your place in line."

Lazarus looked to where the man pointed. Dozens of people were lined up perpendicular to the hillside. If all those people were waiting to meet with Jesus, they'd be here until the sun set.

"You can put me down," Horeb said, "and I will wait with Sarah."

But Lazarus had come this far. He had no idea how long the wait would be for Horeb to spend time with Jesus, but Lazarus wanted to be there when he did.

CHAPTER THREE
Martha

MARTHA PACED BEFORE THE DOOR of her sister's bedchamber. When she'd found Mary outside the synagogue the other night, Martha had barely held her patience together. First, Mary wasn't to be outside after dark. Not because of risk to body and limb but because virtuous women needed to keep their reputations intact.

Yet Martha had kept her reprimands silent all the way home, and then all through Sabbath evening, and all the next day, so that Leah wouldn't be distressed by an argument between the sisters on the Sabbath. When Lazarus was gone, the burden rested heavier upon all of them, and Martha didn't want to add to that. Keeping her frustrations inside was best for the extended family.

Now awake since the first silver gleam of dawn, Martha couldn't rest, couldn't relax. What if someone had seen Mary? The last thing their family needed was to be the center of village gossip right before the official betrothal ceremony and banquet. A tarnish on Mary's name would bring disgrace upon the entire family.

And Martha couldn't allow that to happen. She needed Mary to understand how close she'd brought the family to ruin.

Martha's patience was no longer hers to hold, and she cracked open the door to Mary's bedchamber. Unlike the evening before when Martha had found it empty, the room was now occupied. But instead of finding her sister still asleep, Mary sat on a cushion near the window, bent over a scroll in her lap.

For a moment, Martha second-guessed her rehearsed reprimand. Mary's explanation about being outside the synagogue so she could listen to Elder Gideon's reading of the words of Isaiah had seemed innocent enough, but Mary knew Lazarus wouldn't approve of such actions while he was traveling. This concerned Martha.

Mary was so engrossed in her reading that she didn't even look up when Martha entered. Perhaps their father had been remiss in teaching Mary to read like the boys in the village. Now, it seemed that Mary spent every spare moment focused on something other than her duties.

Martha crossed to the platform bed and sat on the corner, and only then did her sister lift her head.

At seventeen, Mary was past the typical age of becoming betrothed, but the death of their father had thrown the entire family into mourning. Besides, the man whom their parents had their eye on for Mary's husband had married another in the interim. So now Mary should be more than ready to take the next step in her life—to become a wife and mother and manage a household under her new mother-in-law's tutelage.

Most young women would be more invested in whom they were to marry and anxious to move forward in life. Not Mary. She loved her reading and writing and didn't seem to mind passing time without a spouse.

"Mary," Martha said in a quiet tone.

Mary jerked her chin up, her hazel eyes rounding. Her oval face pinked as she quickly rolled up the scroll she held. "I didn't hear you awaken, sister."

"I'm not sure if I slept."

At this, Mary lowered her eyes. "I told you I am sorry for not letting Leah know where I was going."

Martha exhaled a slow breath. "Being sorry for a mistake is one thing, but deliberately disobeying is another. You sneaked out of our home, the one Lazarus now provides for us. What do you think he would say about your actions last night?"

Mary glanced up, panic darting across her features. "You aren't going to tell him, are you?"

Yes. The answer was yes, but then Martha wondered if she could use this as leverage in her favor. "I haven't decided yet." She raised her hand before Mary could start her pleading. "What if someone saw you sneaking around in the dark? You must understand how serious the consequences could have been. Do you think Isaac would want to marry a woman if she was suspected of secretly meeting someone else? Even if he believed your story, he still has his own reputation to think of."

Mary's mouth dropped open, then she clamped it shut, her eyes no longer full of remorse but fire.

But Martha had to be frank no matter how harsh it sounded.

"I am no harlot," Mary said in a tight tone. "And for anyone to think so or say so is a sin upon *their* heads."

"Perhaps." Martha was glad Mary's response had been passionate. "But you need to understand that your actions affect not only you and your future with Isaac but our brother's family as well."

Mary smoothed back a section of her long dark hair that had fallen over her shoulders. At home, she wore her hair unbound. Martha had never gotten used to that, being a married woman, and now that she was a widow, she continued in her formal habit of wearing a scarf about her head indoors and outdoors.

"Don't tell Lazarus," Mary whispered. "I won't do it again."

Martha didn't move for a moment, didn't respond. "I won't tell him," she finally said with a sigh. "At least not yet, but I might have to tell him if someone saw us last night."

Mary nodded, then swiped at her cheek. A tear had fallen, and Martha looked away. Now wasn't the time for compassion. The villagers would not extend any understanding, so Martha had to be the firm one upholding the rules within the home.

"Now, we must help Leah with the meal preparations today," Martha said. "She is putting on a feast to celebrate our brother's return. Then once we've done her bidding, we'll turn our attention to preparing for your banquet. We have only three more days."

Mary swiped at another tear, then rose to her feet and carried the scroll to her table. "I will be done in a few moments," she said in a contrite tone. "Thank you for watching over me."

"I'll see you soon," Martha said over the tightness in her throat. She headed out of the room and upstairs to her own living quarters. Reprimanding an adult woman was not something she wanted to be doing first thing in the morning. And she, along with Leah, would be more than happy when Lazarus returned.

Martha found Leah in the cooking room dealing with a fussy four-year-old. Naomi was sitting at the table, huge tears rolling down her cheeks as she clutched at her cloth doll.

"What's the matter with Naomi?" Martha asked her sister-in-law in a low tone.

"She doesn't feel well," Leah said. "She was restless all night, and I don't know who slept less."

Martha then noticed that Leah looked tired as well. Violet circles edged her eyes, and her normally smooth bun was frayed.

Martha crossed to little Naomi and sat on the bench next to her. Placing her hand on her cheek, Martha found it warm, nearly hot. "What's wrong, little bean?"

Nathaniel had called Naomi "little bean" since she was a babe, saying she looked like one. The nickname had stuck.

"My throat is scratched," Naomi said, her brown eyes imploring, "and there's fire in my head."

Martha heard the hoarseness in the child's voice. She slipped an arm about Naomi's shoulders and pulled her close. "I'm very sorry you feel so sick." She glanced at Leah, who was watching them with pursed lips.

"I can keep her in my room for the day and night," Martha said. "You don't want to get her illness, and Lazarus will be exhausted when he returns tonight."

Leah's expression remained worried. "You might fall ill, and the banquet is in a few days."

"I will be fine," Martha said. Although she couldn't exactly promise such a thing, it seemed she was the one with the strongest constitution in the family. It had been a long time since she'd been ill.

Leah rested a hand on her large belly as she paused for a moment in her work. "Thank you."

"Do you want to sleep in my bed?" Martha asked Naomi.

The little girl nodded solemnly.

"All right. Now, let's get you some tea for your sore throat." Martha rose from the table and headed outside to the herbal garden that grew alongside the vegetables. She searched through the winter plants but then remembered that she'd given the last healing herbs to her neighbor Eunice, who had been ailing, last week.

She headed back inside. "I need to go to the market after the morning meal to get more herbs."

"Can I come with you?" Naomi asked in a small voice.

"You need to rest," Martha said. "But I won't be gone long."

By the time Martha had helped Leah prepare the morning meal of boiled barley and honey cakes, Rhode and Nathaniel had appeared, dressed and ready for synagogue. Mary still hadn't shown up, and Martha was about to fetch her when Mary came down the stairs.

There was no time for any reprimands about her dalliance. Besides, Mary jumped right into helping with serving and then cleanup.

Martha had to be satisfied with that. She kissed the top of Naomi's head, then hurried out the door.

The morning was still early, but the sun had fully crested the eastern horizon, and the day promised to be cool, though free of clouds or storm. Martha walked in the opposite direction of the boys headed to synagogue. She hoped the herb seller, Josiah, would have the herbs she needed. They'd had plenty of conversations about poultices and teas over the years. Josiah traded with the caravans that passed by Bethany, and he kept up on the knowledge of what to use for the best healing.

"Hello, Martha," Eunice said, coming out of her courtyard, heading in the same direction. "How fares your household?"

Martha glanced at Eunice, a pretty woman about the same age as Martha, except Eunice was married with two boys of her own. Her husband owned the land to the north and managed several large flocks.

"Naomi is ill with a sore throat and fever," Martha said, "and I've run out of herbs. I'm hoping Josiah has what I need."

"Good heavens," Eunice said. "My boys have the same illness. And so does Zachary's little girl."

"Zachary?"

"He runs his flocks on my husband's land."

Martha nodded, now remembering the widower she'd seen at the burial ground the day before. "Something is sweeping through the village, then," she said. "Naomi only has contact with her brothers, so I wonder if Rhode and Nathaniel have something too." She hadn't noticed any symptoms in them at the morning meal, though.

"Oh, and Mary's betrothal banquet," Eunice murmured. "I hope these ill children will recover."

If Martha wasn't worried enough, here was a new challenge. When they reached the market square, she was gratified to see that Josiah was already there.

Other women were crowded around the herb seller's cart. Martha's heart sank as she approached. The conversations buzzing among the women all had one thing in common: their children were sick.

"Martha, we're glad you're here," an older woman, Phebe, said. She had adult children and young grandchildren. "Two of my grandchildren have been ill all night, and Josiah here says we should try these herbs. Is that what you recommend?"

Perhaps because Martha never kept silent about the best remedies to use, many of the village women consulted with her on herb concoctions. "Yes," Martha said. "I've come to purchase them for my niece as well."

Josiah stood on the other side of his cart, his expression one of relief. As a round-faced, stocky man, he always seemed to be perspiring. Today was no different despite the cool weather. Martha knew that some of the women could be skeptical or critical of mixtures, tonics, and poultices, often saying that illness, or even death, was simply Adonai's will.

Martha didn't see it quite that way. Yes, God was all-knowing and all-powerful, but God had also provided herbs to heal and ease ailments.

Josiah raised his hands to stop the women as they congregated about him, demanding the herbs. "Please form a line in the order you arrived."

Arguments broke out as the women shuffled into a line.

When Josiah motioned for Martha to join him at the cart, she did so. "Tell them only one handful per person, or I'll run out."

Martha helped Josiah navigate the purchases, and soon more women in the village showed up. Even Tamara showed up. Despite her ancient age, she managed to participate in village events. She reached a trembling hand toward the pouch Josiah had prepared for her.

"Do you want me to help you home?" Martha asked Tamara. The woman's trembling only increased each time she saw her.

"I will be fine, dearest," Tamara said. "I told my daughter-in-law I'd make the errand. Her three children are ill."

Martha nodded, marveling at Tamara's tenacity. When the line of women finally abated, Martha told Josiah, "I really have to get back to Naomi."

Josiah nodded and pressed a square of cloth against his forehead, then neck. "Thank you for your help. I thought I might be trampled."

Martha smiled, imagining a man the size of Josiah worrying about a few dozen women.

"I was told you have something to reduce fevers," a man's voice said.

Martha and Josiah turned.

Zachary stood there. Martha shouldn't have been surprised; he didn't have a wife to go to the market, so of course, he'd have to come himself. What she was surprised at was how seeing him again, this time up close, made her feel . . . like her stomach had traded places with her heart.

"I've sold a lot of my herbs this morning," Josiah said, "but I've rationed them, so I still have some." He picked up a handful of herbs and carefully wrapped them in loosely woven cloth.

"I've no money, but I can trade for goat cheese," Zachary said, lifting the goatskin he carried, presumably filled with goat cheese.

"That is more than enough," Josiah said. "Is there anything else you need?"

Zachary's gaze connected briefly with Martha's, then moved to the other items in the cart. "I really don't know what to choose. My wife, uh, would have done this. All I want is for Claudia to recover."

"Perhaps Martha can recommend something," Josiah said. "She's well versed in herbs and little girls."

Zachary's dark gaze was back on hers, his eyes the color of tree trunks inside the depths of a forest. "You have daughters?"

"No." Martha quickly shifted her eyes to the items in the cart. "I have no children, but I have a niece and two nephews. You might want some things on hand for your daughter, such as these dried leaves, which can be made into a soothing poultice for insect bites. The herbs Josiah wrapped for you will also make a good tea for upset stomachs."

In her peripheral vision, she saw Zachary nod, his attention still on her. "How do I make the poultice?"

"You dry out the leaves completely, then crush them a little bit and add water until it becomes a paste." Martha lifted her eyes to meet his again. This close, he seemed taller than she'd remembered. He wasn't wearing any sort of head covering this morning, which meant his dark curls gleamed in the morning sun.

Spending most of the day outdoors had darkened his skin, and he seemed well versed in physical labor if his lean, wiry build was any indication.

"Thank you for your help," Zachary said. "I'll take the things she suggested." His dark brows pulled together. "I'm sorry I do not know your name."

"Martha," she said, "sister to Lazarus."

She'd effectively stated her marital status by mentioning her brother instead of a husband.

"I'm Zachary, and my daughter is Claudia."

"I know," Martha said before she could think better of revealing what she knew about him. Besides, she sensed Josiah's interest in their conversation, which meant she should probably take her leave and return to the suffering Naomi.

"Thank you, Josiah," she said quickly, then took a final glance at Zachary. "Best wishes for your daughter's recovery."

Zachary's gaze on her was not reticent in the least. In fact, if Leah or Mary had been with her, they would have surely remarked upon it. And what would they have said? Most likely that Zachary didn't make his curiosity a secret.

As Martha hurried away from the market, the cloth bundle clutched in her hand, she wondered what Zachary was curious about. Her, specifically? Or about her family, about Lazarus? Her brother was one of the wealthier men in the village and hired extra men for seasonal work, and Zachary had given up his land inheritance to start over in Bethany.

Perhaps Zachary was looking for employment during his slower hours?

The main floor of the house was quiet when Martha returned. She'd find where Naomi had settled once the tea was ready.

As Martha bustled around the cooking room preparing the tea, she wondered about Zachary's living quarters. Did he dwell in a tent like some of the other shepherds? Or did he have a more permanent hut? Did his daughter tend sheep all day with him? Did she have any friends to spend time with?

Did Zachary have to neglect his sheep to care for Claudia?

And what concern is it of mine? she chided herself. She carried the cup of tea up the stairs and found Naomi curled up in Mary's bed, sound asleep.

"Leave her," Mary said. "I can watch over her while I do my embroidery."

Martha hesitated, then said, "All right. Have her drink this before it cools. Then she can keep sleeping." She paused. "Other children in the village are ill. We might have a plague."

Mary released the thread she'd been combing through. "I hope not. What about my betrothal banquet?"

"We must pray that all will go well."

CHAPTER FOUR
Lazarus

THE WHISPERS RIPPLED THROUGH THE people waiting along the hillside for their turn to converse with Jesus, and when the whispers reached Lazarus, a shudder crawled through him.

"We must go," he hissed to Horeb and Sarah. "There is a leper ahead of us in line."

Horeb's eyes widened, but Sarah seemed unaffected. Others had moved out of the line and congregated in a circle several paces away, casting furtive glances toward the front of the line.

"Jesus will heal the leper," Sarah said in a quiet tone, "and then he'll be a leper no more."

This had gone too far. Sure, Lazarus had been curious and interested to see if this man named Jesus was a remarkable healer of some sort. But a leper . . . and a blind woman . . . and a man with a lame foot?

"Come, I will carry you back down the hill to safety." Lazarus extended his hand to Horeb, who was sitting on the ground because standing for long periods of time was uncomfortable for him.

But Horeb made no motion to get up off the ground.

"Surely you don't want to risk becoming a leper yourself?" Lazarus said.

Horeb folded his arms. "I have not come all this way to turn around now."

Lazarus looked up the hillside. Several men who seemed to be bodyguards or protectors blocked Lazarus's view of Jesus and the people they'd let through to see Him. Below, the numbers on the hillside had increased. Lower lines had formed, and Lazarus couldn't even guess at all of the ailments this growing crowd had. It was a marvel that some of them had been able to travel here in the first place.

"What is your purpose?" someone said close to Lazarus, who turned to see a man with a thick beard and warm brown eyes.

"Who are you?" Lazarus asked.

"Andrew," the man said. "I'm one of Jesus's Apostles."

"Andrew?" Horeb said with a voice filled with joy. "I have heard of your apostleship. I am Horeb of Jerusalem, and this is our friend Sarah, who is blind."

Sarah placed a hand over her heart. "Andrew, take compassion on an old woman. I have lived many years, and I've yet to see the color of the sky."

Andrew glanced back to Lazarus. "And what do you seek, my friend?"

My friend. Lazarus did not even know this man. "I am but an onlooker."

"He brought us here in his cart," Horeb cut in. "He carried me up the hill, and he refuses to leave our side until he knows all will be well."

Andrew didn't seem surprised at the accolades spoken by Horeb. "Come with me."

At this, Horeb began to scramble to his feet. Lazarus moved quickly to his side to assist him.

"Where are we going?" Lazarus asked. There were still dozens in line ahead of them.

But Andrew didn't answer. He merely linked arms with Sarah and gently led her up the slope, instructing her where the best places were to step. Horeb insisted on walking, but he was in obvious pain, so Lazarus insisted right back that he carry the man.

As they approached a group of men forming a semicircle, one of them turned and saw Andrew. The man stepped aside, and Lazarus followed Andrew into the inner circle. Despite the crowds below on the hillside, this inner circle was quiet, and . . . Lazarus didn't know a word for it. Watchful? Peaceful? Reverent.

A man stood in their midst. This was the man Sarah had proclaimed was Jesus. His dark hair skimmed His shoulders, and Lazarus guessed Him to be near His thirtieth year. The man's gaze shifted, slowly, to the new arrivals. His brown eyes didn't miss a thing but seemed contemplative, despite all the people waiting to see Him.

As he peered at the small group, Lazarus felt unsteady for reasons he couldn't decipher. Yes, Horeb had seemed to grow in weight, but the distance had been short. No one was speaking. Not the circle of men who merely gazed at them, nor the man who seemed to be their leader.

"I have brought Horeb and Sarah to meet Jesus of Nazareth," Lazarus said, not wanting to put Horeb down yet if they still had more climbing to do.

"It's he," Sarah whispered. "It's Jesus of Nazareth."

Lazarus should be used to Sarah's unseeing insight by now, but the hairs on his arms rose at her words because . . . because the man standing before him, with His brown eyes that seemed both all-knowing and compassionate at the same time, was not an ordinary man. Although the thought struck Lazarus with unexpected force, he could in no way explain why he knew this. It was simply a feeling, the strongest feeling he'd ever had.

"I will walk to Him," Horeb said, and Lazarus bent his knees so that Horeb could slide off his back.

Horeb was unsteady, though, and Lazarus grasped the man's upper arm.

"This is Lazarus," Andrew told Jesus. "And he has brought Horeb, who is lame, and Sarah, who is blind. They are not family, but Lazarus has taken it upon himself to bring the pair to meet you."

Andrew's words were simple and accurate, yet Jesus's full attention was caught, and He looked directly at Lazarus.

"Seek ye first the kingdom of God," Jesus said, His gaze seeming to penetrate Lazarus's very soul. "Come unto me."

It almost seemed Jesus was speaking to *him*, Lazarus thought, but that was impossible. Horeb and Sarah were seeking this man, not he.

"May I touch Him?" Sarah said, her voice just above a whisper.

Andrew moved forward with Sarah as she stretched out her hand. Her feet seemed to glide across the rocky slope until she stood directly in front of Jesus. She lifted a knobby hand, her fingers trembling as she brushed the tips against Jesus's sleeve.

"Receive thy sight: thy faith hath saved thee."

Air rushed through Lazarus as if he'd been holding his breath, although he'd done no such thing. Sarah sank to her knees, her entire body trembling now. Lazarus rushed forward, worried that she'd reached her limit and was about to collapse. But instead of collapsing, she grasped the hem of Jesus's robe and kissed it.

"Thank you, dear Lord," she whispered in the watchful stillness of the circle. "My sight has been restored."

Lazarus paused, unable to move. Sarah turned her head toward him, and her blue-gray eyes were clearer now. Tears streaked her cheeks, but they weren't tears of sorrow. Not any longer.

"You are Lazarus?" she said, her voice stronger now, her gaze firmly settled upon him.

"I am," Lazarus choked out. His throat had closed, and his heart was galloping like a horse in a chariot race.

"Thank you, my friend," Sarah said. Then she was kissing the hem of his robe.

"No, Sarah, you must not worship me," Lazarus said, grasping her shoulders. "We must only worship . . ."

He couldn't finish because he again felt Jesus's gaze on him. When Lazarus lifted his chin, he saw the edges of a smile in Jesus's expression. Lazarus swallowed, his throat feeling as if he'd inhaled fire.

Before Lazarus could wrap his mind around the fact that Sarah's blindness had somehow been cured, and by what means, he didn't know . . . Jesus turned to Horeb.

"I've had this affliction since my birth," Horeb said, a tremor in his voice. "It has been the greatest curse of my life."

Jesus merely watched as Horeb drew closer. And when Horeb sank onto his knees before the man, Jesus touched Horeb's cheek and said, "Son, thy sins be forgiven thee."

Lazarus stared at Jesus. Who was he to extend forgiveness for sins?

And then that thought fled Lazarus's mind when Jesus added, "Rise up and walk."

Horeb grasped Jesus's outstretched hand, and Lazarus expected him to hobble to his feet. Instead, Horeb rose to his full height, steady and sure.

Turning in a full circle, Horeb grinned. Then he took several steps and laughed. He bent, then straightened, then bent again. His face was alight with joy as he shook his foot, then took turns hopping on one foot, then the other.

Watching Horeb celebrate, Lazarus was sure he'd awaken from this odd dream in a matter of minutes. But none of this was a dream. Horeb was walking like a man who'd never seen an injury in his life. And Sarah . . . she turned in slow circles, gazing at the sky and the trees, then stooped to pick up a rock and turn it over in her hand. Her eyes shone with appreciation, curiosity, gratitude, and joy.

Lazarus could no longer hold back his tears, and he couldn't swallow against the tautness in his throat. Before his very eyes, this man named Jesus had somehow healed two people of lifetime ailments.

"Make way," someone said, and the circle parted as another man entered.

The man's face was full of sores, and his arms and hands were bandaged. His gait was slow, which told Lazarus that his legs and feet might be equally damaged, for this man suffered from leprosy.

Lazarus had never been this close to the unclean before, and instinctively, he moved back, nearly bumping into Andrew.

But Andrew only rested a hand on Lazarus's shoulder and said, "All will be well, Lazarus. You will see."

Sarah and Horeb seemed to have no qualms about a leper in their midst. And neither did Jesus, nor the other men in the circle.

The leper bowed his head as he approached Jesus. "Lord, if thou wilt, thou canst make me clean."

Without flinching away or even seeming appalled, Jesus placed a hand on the man's turban. "I will; be thou clean."

The leper's shoulders slumped, and Lazarus realized he was crying. With joy.

In amazement, Lazarus watched the leper pull off the wraps along his arms, then tug off his soiled turban. He turned with a smile, a smile that wasn't crooked, marked with sores, or showing any sort of deformity.

The man wasn't old at all but likely only two decades. And the leprosy was gone. Absolutely gone.

Lazarus couldn't comprehend fully what he was seeing, what he was witnessing, but three people had been healed before his very eyes. Tears streaked his cheeks, unchecked and unbidden.

"How can I thank you, my good man?" Horeb said, clapping him on the shoulder. His face was still glowing with pure joy.

Lazarus turned his watery gaze upon Horeb. "It is I . . . who must thank you. I do not know how to explain what I have seen today. But . . . I . . . am in awe."

Horeb grinned as he brushed at the tears on his own face. "If it weren't for you, I would have never made it here in time." He motioned toward his healed foot, lifting it from the ground and rotating it. "No pain. No tightness. Fully healed. I feel like I could run all the way back to Jerusalem."

Lazarus chuckled. "I do not doubt it, my friend."

More people entered the circle. The blind, the maimed, the diseased.

"Come," Andrew said, joining Lazarus and Horeb. "We will let others through."

Lazarus took another look at Jesus, who was speaking to a woman holding an infant with a deformity about his ear. He wanted to sit at the man's side and observe all he did.

Sarah had moved out of the circle and was speaking to people still waiting in line, telling them of her healing.

"Lazarus," someone said behind him, and he turned to see Andrew the Apostle.

"At dusk, we are traveling to a home in Galilee to spend the night," Andrew said. "We are in need of a cart. Would you be willing to take Jesus and a few of us? Jesus will be exhausted from His work here today. As you can see, there are many more who need His attention."

Lazarus could only stare at Andrew because no words would come. He was both incredulous and humbled at the request. Yes, this would put him even farther behind in his journey back to Bethany. But to have the chance to learn more about Jesus? Slowly, he nodded. "Yes, yes, I will take you."

Andrew smiled. "Thank you, good man."

Lazarus dipped his head, his heart racing at this opportunity.

As Andrew walked away, Horeb released a rushed breath. "You have been chosen."

Lazarus watched Andrew's retreating form. "Surely they own their own cart. A man such as Jesus?" He looked past Horeb. There were no longer hundreds on the hillside. The numbers had to be more than a thousand by now. All people wanting to see Jesus, the Master Healer.

"Jesus has no riches in this world," Horeb said in a soft voice. "His wealth is in His teachings alone."

The words struck Lazarus with power, and he knew it would take time for him to truly comprehend them. Lazarus studied Horeb, gazing at his left foot, which was now equal in appearance to his right foot. "You are truly healed?"

"I am," Horeb said, his mouth curving into a smile. "If I cannot run all the way to Jerusalem right now, do you want to watch me run up and down the hill?"

A laugh escaped Lazarus. "Perhaps another time. I should check on my donkeys and make sure they are fed. It seems I've been commissioned for another duty."

Horeb continued smiling. "Bless you and your family, Lazarus."

Lazarus nodded, hoping his wife and children wouldn't worry too much about him. He'd been delayed before—it was the nature of his industry and traveling the roads of Palestine. Right now, he only felt peace at his decision to accept Andrew's offer. Lazarus would be headed home soon enough, and this hillside teeming with people was something he was sure he'd never witness again in his life.

Setting off down the hillside, he passed groups of people, and he couldn't help but overhear their conversations. Most looked as if they'd made great sacrifices to travel here, just like Horeb and Sarah. As Lazarus neared the base of the hill and his cart came into sight, he noticed a cluster of men—Pharisees as well as scribes—their clothing fine and distinguished, setting them apart from the general population.

Lazarus slowed his step, curious that such a variety of people had come.

No matter. Lazarus had no business with them. After he secured his cart and looked after his donkeys, he studied the increasing crowd. There were well over a thousand people now, perhaps even double that. As far as Lazarus could see along the road, more and more were coming. And no one was leaving.

Lazarus started up the hillside once again, pausing to hear stories of miracles among the conversations of the people. Entire families were present, babes in arms, the elderly and infirm. Lazarus wondered where all of these people were from.

"There you are," Horeb said, coming toward him when Lazarus was nearly to the area where he'd last seen the man. "Jesus is going to feed the crowd, then teach us principles of the new gospel."

"New gospel?" Lazarus echoed. "And how will He feed such a large crowd?" He could see no massive collection of baskets anywhere.

"The new gospel is the law of Moses fulfilled," Horeb said. He pointed down the hillside. "See those men? The scribes and the Pharisees?"

"I passed by them earlier," Lazarus said.

"They are not happy with the teachings of Jesus," Horeb said. "Andrew told me that Jesus and His Apostles are followed everywhere by men such as these. It's as if they're spies."

Lazarus frowned. "Have they threatened harm to Jesus?"

"No harm has come to Him yet," Horeb said. "But we must hurry if we want a spot near Jesus so that we might hear His words firsthand. Andrew said they have seven fish and several loaves of bread that will be distributed among the people soon."

Lazarus released a light chuckle. "Only a dozen will be fed, then, and children at that."

Horeb rested a hand on Lazarus's shoulder as they moved farther up the hillside, not for support but because he had moved closer and lowered his voice. "That's just the thing, my friend. We are about to witness another miracle. Feeding four thousand people with seven fishes and a handful of loaves of bread is a simple matter to Jesus of Nazareth."

CHAPTER FIVE
Mary

MARY PULLED HER KNEES TO her chest as she sat on the village wall that overlooked the road leading north to Galilee. Her brother, Lazarus, was more than a day late from his travels. Leah was in a frenzy. Naomi was ill. Martha was fretting over all the illnesses in the village. Rhode and Nathaniel were avoiding being home as much as possible. And Mary was . . . distracted.

Her betrothal banquet would be the day after tomorrow. In the presence of the older adult males in each family, she would make promises to Isaac. Then the two extended families would eat and celebrate. Next, preparations would begin for the wedding and then the marriage . . . and then what? Mary would instantly become a mother to Isaac's two children from his first marriage.

She squeezed her eyes shut as she thought of Isaac's most recent words to her when he'd come by the house to inquire if Lazarus was home. Mary had been in the courtyard taking a rare moment to sit down and look over the scroll she'd practiced writing upon. She hadn't heard Isaac approach.

Although Isaac was a kind man, he was always serious. Perhaps it was because he was a widower. Had he been more cheerful with his first wife? Mary wondered if she'd ever seen him truly smile. And although his words were said in a mild tone, they could still cut to the core.

"Soon you will no longer concern yourself with matters that belong only to men," Isaac had said. "My children will keep you very busy."

Mary had quickly rolled up the scroll and tucked it inside her robe. Her cheeks had grown hot, not because she'd been caught sitting and reading but because she always stayed busy and didn't need him to remind her that his children would take even more of her time. Mary always had plenty to do, and a few stolen moments to sit and read were sometimes her only pleasure.

That thought should have made her wonder if she really wanted to be married as custom dictated.

The answer was yes. Every woman desired marriage and children. Hers was not to be a life under her brother's roof and days dictated by a sister-in-law. But in Isaac's home, she would be beholden to her mother-in-law, and yes, to Isaac's children, and soon her own.

"I am only on a small break," Mary had said, feeling the need to defend herself. "I've been awake since dawn, helping Leah with Naomi, who has been ill."

Isaac was only a handspan taller than Mary, yet he had the habit of slouching in almost everything he did, so he seemed to be eye level with her. When he'd spoken next, his light-brown eyes peered at her, his brow creased. "So many children are ill, but not mine. My mother has been careful with their health and making sure they are never disobedient."

Mary wanted to argue and tell Isaac that Naomi hadn't been disobedient either. She'd heard discussions about the connections between obedience and health, but she'd also heard the arguments against it. Yes, she made it a habit of listening outside the synagogue to the teachings of the elders many more times than anyone in her family realized. A few weeks ago, a traveling Pharisee spent two days in the Bethany synagogue, and Mary had listened as much as she dared.

And now, Mary had told Leah she'd see if she could spot Lazarus on his way home. She couldn't sit on the wall and wait for too long, but it felt nice to have the cool breeze and the faint bleating of the flocks on the hillside beyond as her only companions.

Lazarus's presence would bring calm and peace back into the household. Mary had also hoped to speak to him about Isaac because before he'd left the courtyard that morning, Isaac had said that he expected her to leave all scrolls behind when they married. The very idea had set Mary's pulse skittering like a darting mouse.

Lazarus didn't mind her studies, did he? He'd always seemed neutral about it. And it was their father who'd taught her to read in the first place. He'd tried to teach Martha, but she had only stayed through a couple of lessons before saying she had other things to spend her time on.

Leah had never commented on it. Martha had certainly been vocal but only when she felt like Mary was being slow to fulfill her duties. Martha had never told her to quit. Although Martha was her sister, she'd been more like a mother all these years. And it was during Martha's brief marriage that Mary had become more and more involved in studies, using them to hold off the loneliness as well as satisfy the many questions that wouldn't seem to leave her alone.

Mary knew that, going into her marriage, new expectations would have to be met. But did her desires count for nothing? Were her desires wrong in the first place? Shouldn't she desire a husband, children, and serving her in-laws above all else? Mary rubbed at her temples, which had started to throb. She was seventeen, and all of the young women in the village her age were married, most with a child.

Would taking her concerns to Lazarus be out of line? She couldn't live under her brother's roof forever. And what about Martha? She'd married and was now widowed. Mary knew her sister was still sad. Yes, Mary saw it in the moments when Martha didn't think anyone was paying attention to her.

If Mary shared her concerns with Martha, she'd just tell Mary it was time to take on the responsibilities of an adult woman. So here she sat, waiting until it was time to accept her fate. She straightened when she saw a cart come into view on the crest of the hill. The two donkeys were familiar, and the man driving those donkeys was undoubtedly her brother.

Mary slid off the wall, her pulse leaping in anticipation. Lazarus was back. He was home. At last. She didn't run to tell the good news to Leah but instead went to greet him. She hurried along the road toward the approaching cart. But another form appeared from the cart, and Mary realized a man was walking behind it. He was leading a donkey by a rope. The man wasn't anyone she recognized. At least not anyone from Bethany.

Mary knew Lazarus did business with many others in his travels, so perhaps this was another trader. As Mary neared the cart, Lazarus lifted his hand in greeting. His smile was broad, and Mary smiled back. Why couldn't Isaac be more like her brother and not be so serious all the time? There were things to celebrate in life, such as the safe return of her brother.

She couldn't help but break into a run, and in moments, Lazarus stepped down from the cart and swept her into his arms.

"You are happy to see me?" Lazarus said with a chuckle, holding her tight, then drawing away.

"Yes, brother," Mary said. "You have been delayed?" Only then did she glance at the man who walked along the other side of the cart.

She guessed him to be only a few years older than she, and upon closer inspection, she was struck with how shabby he seemed in his threadbare robe, no shoes, and hair that looked like it had never been washed. Not much above the station of a beggar. Had Lazarus brought a beggar to Bethany? Was he diseased? She quickly scanned the rest of his person but didn't see any evidence of disease or other signs of being among the unclean. The donkey he led wasn't much better off either.

"This is Horeb," Lazarus said, extending a hand to the young man. "We met in Galilee."

"Hello. Nice to meet you," Horeb said in a warm and friendly tone. "Are you Mary or Martha?"

"Mary."

Horeb's smile was crooked, and there was something about the curiosity and appreciation in his expression that had Mary looking quickly away. No one looked at Mary like that anymore in their village. Not when the men knew she was spoken for by Isaac. Not when the men knew her brother and his protectiveness. She'd almost forgotten what it was like to have a man openly admire her.

But this man named Horeb was a stranger to Bethany. Still, he should assume she was married or, at the very least, betrothed, which she nearly was. What had her brother told this man if he already knew the names of his sisters?

She was curious about him too, only because she wondered where he was from and why he was traveling with her brother.

Lazarus rested a hand on her shoulder as they continued walking along the road. "How fares Leah and the boys? How is my little bean?"

Right, Mary should be sharing the latest news. "Naomi has been ill, but today she is looking better. Many children in the village have been ailing, though, and Martha has been giving instructions on herbal remedies."

"I have no doubt Martha has been helpful," Lazarus said. "But I'm glad to hear Naomi is doing better. And Leah?"

"She is working too hard and ignores Martha's pleas to take a rest."

Lazarus chuckled. "I am not surprised. Leah only rests when she's asleep, and that is when she worries."

Mary wanted to ask her brother about what Isaac had said to him, but she couldn't very well do that with a stranger walking with them. Would Horeb go to the inn at Bethany? Was he traveling on to Jerusalem? He made no effort to join in the conversation.

They reached the village wall, where Mary had been waiting, when she finally glanced behind her. Horeb was gazing across the fields, a thoughtful expression on his face. Before Mary could look forward again, he caught her glance. The slight tilt of his mouth in acknowledgment sent Mary's mind spinning with questions again.

She looked at Lazarus and scrambled for something to say that would cover up her distraction. "Was your journey successful?"

Lazarus looked down at her with a soft smile. "Oh, Mary. I can't wait to tell the family of my amazing experiences and Horeb's. As soon as I am settled at home, we'll fetch Rhode and Nathaniel from their lessons, and I will share what happened."

Mary didn't know how to respond to that. Horeb was part of an amazing experience? The back of her neck warmed, and she was almost certain the stranger was looking at her. As they moved through the village, Lazarus was greeted by several people, and he took the time to introduce Horeb to each of them. When they saw Benjamin, a village man who'd severely broken his leg the year before and now walked with a cane, Lazarus made it a point that the two men meet.

Horeb was friendly and courteous, smiling freely yet not giving out any more information about his identity. This only made Mary more curious about him, if only from an interest standpoint. Would Lazarus direct him to the inn after sharing whatever their amazing experience had been?

"I can fetch Rhode and Nathaniel," Mary offered. She might have to interrupt their lessons, but perhaps she could glean a little information beforehand. Besides, she needed to get her thoughts organized. Horeb's unexpected presence had scrambled them.

Before Lazarus could say much more than a word of agreement, Mary veered off, heading toward the village synagogue. As she approached the small building with stone benches inside, a sense of excitement tingled through her. A place that was a house of learning was fascinating to her. She moved around the side of the building and took up one of her usual spots below a window to listen. A few moments wouldn't hurt before she fetched her nephews.

She could hear the clear tone of the instructor, one of the village elders, Elder Gideon. He was speaking about the prophet Micah. Mary already knew that he was a prophet who lived at the same time as Amos, Hosea, and Isaiah. Micah's book told of how the judgment of God would fall upon Samaria and Jerusalem due to the sinners within those cities. And, eventually, God would restore them.

Then Elder Gideon shifted to speaking about the city of Bethlehem and how it would be the birthplace of a ruler greater than David. This always gave Mary something to think about. Not many rulers could be greater than David.

A woman slowed as she passed the synagogue, glancing over at Mary. It was Eunice. Mary waved and said hello, then felt like she couldn't spy beneath the window any longer. So she went to the entrance and told the young scribe there that she was seeking her nephews. A few moments later, Rhode and Nathaniel came out, questions in their eyes.

"Your father is home," Mary told them, "and he wants to speak with the family."

Nathaniel grinned, but Rhode, the more serious, elder brother, frowned. Surely he realized this was unusual.

"Is Father well?" Rhode asked. He was a gangly youth, but his voice had started to deepen.

"He's very well," Mary said. "And he seems very excited to speak with the family, so don't worry."

The lines on Rhode's forehead faded, and he nodded.

Mary walked with her nephews and asked them what they'd learned that day in their lessons. But before they could explain much, Martha came around the corner, hurrying toward them.

She looked from Mary to their nephews.

"What's going on?" Martha said, her brow furrowed deep.

It was unusual for the boys to be walking through the village in the middle of a lesson day.

"Lazarus has returned, and he said he wants to share an experience with the entire family," Mary explained.

"Is everything well with him?" Martha asked.

"Yes, but he's asked for the family to gather."

Martha gave a faint nod. "All right. But first, I need your help, Mary. It's urgent." Without waiting for a reply, Martha turned to their nephews. "Tell your father that Mary and I will be back shortly. We've gone to help a sick child."

CHAPTER SIX
Martha

MARTHA HOPED HER EXPLANATION TO Mary would be enough for now because she didn't want to have to give too much information yet. She didn't know herself what would happen exactly, but she knew Zachary's daughter was very ill.

This morning, she'd gone to the market to pick up a few things when Josiah told her that Zachary had been back too. He'd taken his daughter to the village healer, but the healer refused to treat the young girl, saying there was nothing he could do because she had an unclean spirit inside of her. Josiah had provided another type of herb, yet he, too, was at a loss.

So Martha had hurried home to gather a few supplies, then searched for Mary, who was nowhere to be found. When Leah told her that Mary had been watching for Lazarus, Martha headed out of the house.

Now she was guiding her confused sister through the back streets of the village so that they wouldn't be stopped and questioned. It wasn't every day that Martha paid a visit to a widower, and she couldn't do it alone.

Waiting for her brother to accompany her might be too late. She'd never seen Josiah so worried before.

"Martha, slow down," Mary protested. "Where are we going?"

Martha paused, her breathing heavy, as she surveyed where they were exactly. They'd reached the first fields outside of Bethany. A copse of trees sat not too far off, and it was a location Martha knew was used by the shepherds for afternoon breaks from the hot sun. No one was there now because the winter sun remained distant.

She shifted her basket onto her other hip. "Remember the man who works for Eunice and Joel?"

"Zachary the widower?"

"Yes," Martha said. "His daughter is very ill. The healer doesn't think she'll live much longer."

Mary took a step back. "What if the disease is catching?"

Martha had considered that, of course. But she felt compelled to help. "You don't have to come inside where they live. I just need you with me for propriety's sake."

Mary's brow lifted, but then she nodded. "All right. Where do they live?"

"I'm not exactly sure," Martha confessed. "I couldn't very well ask around or rumors might start. So I was hoping to get this far and see a tent or a hut, then go from there."

"Perhaps beyond the trees?" Mary suggested. "Or on the other side of that hill?"

Martha set off again, gripping the basket tightly so that she could transport some of her tenseness there. They trudged through the copse of trees, and to her surprise, they came upon a tent tucked into the hillside just down the slope.

"Is this his place?" Mary asked.

"I hope so." Martha slowed her approach, looking for any evidence that a man and his daughter occupied the tent. It could belong to another shepherd entirely.

But then her attention was caught by the sound of crying. A young girl crying, to be exact.

Martha quickened her pace again, Mary keeping up, worry in her own expression.

"Zachary? Claudia?" Martha called when she stepped up to the tent flap that closed off the entrance. "It's Martha, sister of Lazarus."

The crying girl quieted, and the flap moved over to reveal a stooped Zachary as he peered out at them.

"Goodness, are you ill too?" Mary blurted out.

Martha's voice was stuck somewhere in her throat. Zachary wore no turban, his dark curls were wild, and his face was shadowed with exhaustion. The sound of his daughter's whimpers could be heard more clearly now.

"What are you . . . ?" Zachary's gaze cut from Martha to Mary, then to the basket.

"I've come with some remedies for your daughter," Martha said. "Josiah told me what the healer said."

Zachary stepped out of the tent, straightening to his full height, and rubbed a hand over his face. "The healer says she is possessed and there is nothing he can do." His dark eyes were like deep wells of pain. "If the healer can't help her, I don't think anyone can."

Martha knew he wasn't saying this to be patronizing because she recognized the hopelessness and grim acceptance in those dark eyes of his. Here was a man who had done all he could, yet it wasn't enough.

"Martha knows more than the village healer," Mary said. "She's helped many people when the healer couldn't."

Martha's chest expanded at the compliment, but it was hardly something to be proud of. She wasn't trying to best a well-respected man.

"Is this true?" Zachary rasped, his tone holding the faintest bit of hope.

"It's true." Martha lifted her chin to fortify herself against any scrutiny despite the fact that her stomach clenched with doubt. "Although I don't take credit. Prayers are also a big part of the healing process."

Zachary's eyes searched hers. "Are you going to tell me that my little girl's suffering is God's will?"

"No." Martha stepped forward. "I do believe that God has given us herbs to use for our benefit, but He also expects us to have faith."

Zachary closed his eyes and released a slow breath. When he opened his eyes again, they bore into Martha's.

"Are you not afraid that my daughter is possessed?"

Martha's chest hitched, but she kept her chin lifted. "I am not."

Zachary's shoulders visibly sagged. "I will do anything . . ." His voice cracked. "I will give you whatever you need in payment if you can help my daughter."

"No payment necessary," Martha said around a tight throat.

He stared at her for a moment, then stepped aside, holding open the tent flap. "Please come in."

Martha glanced at Mary. "Alert me if anyone comes into sight."

Mary nodded.

The interior of the tent was dim, but Martha's eyes quickly adjusted. The one room was simply furnished. A single table contained the remains of a meal. There were no chairs, just a couple of ratty cushions. No platform bed but two mats; upon one was Claudia's small form huddled beneath a rug.

The girl's dark hair spilled across the mat below her, and her face was as pale as the winter moon. Her eyes were closed, and her delicate lids fluttered in her sleep. It was not the sleep of a healthy little girl but of someone who was experiencing pain and distress.

Zachary had followed her inside and now hovered a few feet behind her.

"What has she complained about?" Martha said in a quiet tone, not wanting to disturb the child yet. It was hard to believe how some could say an unclean spirit resided within this girl's small body.

"She complains about pain in her stomach," he said. "And she's been crying in her sleep, so not even sleep has brought her relief. When she's awake, it's much worse. She says a lion is stalking her and trying to catch her."

Martha exhaled. Either the girl was out of her mind or she was hallucinating because of her illness. "Can she keep food down?"

"Yes, but she refuses to eat." Zachary gestured to the lone table and the meal remnants upon it.

"What have you fed her?"

"Bits of flatbread, some cooked vegetables, and boiled barley."

Martha crossed to the table and set her basket upon it. Then she drew out an herbal root. "Can you start a cooking fire and heat up water for tea, then steep this root?"

"Of course." Zachary headed to another opening in the tent, drew the flap aside, then stepped to where he had a cooking fire that needed to be stoked to life.

While he worked, Martha crossed to Claudia and knelt beside the child. Placing her hand on the girl's forehead, Martha was pleased to find that it was clammy to the touch but not burning like she'd feared. Perhaps the worst of the fever had already passed?

Claudia stirred with a whimper, and Martha lifted her hand. When Claudia settled again, Martha drew the rug from her small body, gazing at the child's limbs. Nothing seemed to be bruised or discolored. No sores dotted her arms or legs or feet. Her skin prickled with goose pimples at the temperature change, so Martha replaced the rug.

Noises from Zachary's preparation of the tea were the only sounds in the tent. Martha felt Zachary's gaze on her as she did the examination, but neither of them spoke, and there were no words needed.

Claudia's lips were dry and starting to crack, and the skin about her eyes and mouth had taken on a slight yellow tinge.

Martha wanted to check one more thing. She gently pinched the skin between her neck and shoulder, and as Martha had suspected, the skin stayed pinched for a moment after release.

Claudia's eyes fluttered open, but she didn't make a sound. The child's eyes seemed lackluster and not entirely focused.

Martha hadn't even heard Zachary approach, but suddenly he was there, kneeling on the other side of his daughter.

"What do you think?" he whispered.

"She has no fever," Martha said. "But she needs nourishment, even if we have to force-feed her."

"She's refused everything," he said. "She's bitten me when I've tried to feed her. I don't see how we can get her to eat or drink."

"We will do it for her."

Zachary's brows drew together. "How?"

Martha rose to her feet and brushed at her tunic. "Together." She crossed to the table and drew out the boiled barley she'd brought from home and added more water to it from the goatskin inside the basket. She stirred the broth, making it very watery.

"The tea should be ready," she told Zachary. "We'll start with that."

Zachary arose and fetched the pot of tea in which the root had been steeping. He poured the steaming liquid into a clay cup.

Martha held out her hand for the cup, and he gave it to her, their eyes connecting for a brief instant. Zachary's gaze was full of questions and hope.

"You will hold her from behind and make sure she doesn't try to knock away the cup or turn her head."

"All right." Zachary moved to the mat and knelt at the top of it, then drew his daughter into a half-sitting position, holding her against him.

Claudia's eyes flew open. "No! No!" she cried out, struggling against her father's grip.

"Don't let her go," Martha said in a sharp voice, although her hands were trembling.

Claudia began to jerk and kick, so Martha knelt over her legs. "Hold her arms."

Zachary did so, but Claudia had started to thrash her head and cry.

Martha spoke louder than the girl's crying. "You are very ill, Claudia," she said. "Your body needs liquids or else you will not recover."

Claudia fought against her father's hold, but he was much stronger, especially with Martha there to support his actions.

Martha grasped the child's chin with her hand. "Open your mouth, Claudia, and drink some tea." In her other hand, the tea sloshed and spilled over the side of the cup. But that was only a small deterrent.

She tipped the cup, and part of the tea entered the girl's mouth.

Claudia began to spit, but surely a little had gotten down her throat.

"Calm down, Claudia," Martha said. "You need to drink more."

"The lion is going to get me," Claudia cried out, her eyes wild, her body thrashing.

"The lion can't touch us," Martha said. "Drink this, and he'll go away."

Claudia stilled for the briefest of moments. Martha used it to her advantage and poured more tea into her mouth. Claudia swallowed an entire mouthful. Then she started to thrash again.

"You're doing better," Martha said to both Claudia and Zachary. "The lion can't get you if you drink this. It will repel him." She tipped the cup again, keeping a firm hold of Claudia's chin.

The young girl spat it out, but there had been progress at least. And Claudia's strength was lessening.

"Release her for a moment," Martha told Zachary.

He eased his grip, his own hands trembling from distress at having to hold his daughter down. Claudia sagged against her father, and Martha touched the girl's cheek. "See, the lion has left."

Claudia's eyes searched about the tent.

"He's not here anymore," Martha said. "Drink more tea so he'll stay away."

Claudia opened her mouth and drank several swallows.

"Very good," Martha said. "You're a brave girl. Much braver than any lion I know."

Claudia nodded, and her eyes slid shut, her body exhausted from all of her fighting.

"We'll let her sleep now," Martha said, backing away, then standing.

Relief etched across Zachary's face as he settled Claudia onto the mat. He joined Martha at the table, where she placed a cloth over the bowl of broth. "It is too soon to try the broth," she said. "But I'll be back as soon as I can, and we'll feed her more tea."

She glanced at Zachary to see him gazing at her with astonishment.

"You're coming back?"

"You can't very well get her to eat or drink while she is still hallucinating," Martha said. "It takes two adults. Do you have someone else to help?"

"No," he said in a soft tone. "There is no one else."

Martha gave a firm nod. "I'll be back as soon as I am able. If she becomes lucid at all, give her more tea, but don't try to force her until I return. She could hurt herself or you."

Zachary only stared at her, his eyes intense.

"She is not possessed by an unclean spirit," Martha said. "She is hallucinating, and that will go away once her illness passes. So do not fear, Zachary. All will be well. I will return before the sun sets."

"You don't know what this means to me. She's only seven, and I cannot lose her so young." Zachary's throat worked, and he seemed about to tell her something more, but then he only said, "Thank you."

The words were simple, and ones Martha had heard often all her life. But Zachary's thank-you somehow struck Martha's heart in a deep place she'd kept hidden since her husband's death.

Once Martha was out of the tent, she inhaled the cool air. The child needed a lot of care, and she knew Zachary was still overwhelmed. Martha herself felt shaky at the experience, but she'd seen dehydration before, and she knew that hallucinations could result. The poor child was very ill, but there was a cure. It would just be agonizing to get through. But now, she had to return home to hear about her brother's journey and to act like she wasn't leaving a piece of her heart behind in this small tent.

"Martha," Mary said, rising from her perch on a boulder. Her beautiful eyes were wide with curiosity. "What happened in there? Is she going to be all right?"

Martha told her sister her predictions. "I must come back in a few hours," she said. "Will you come with me? Zachary can't do this on his own."

"Yes, I'll come."

The two sisters linked arms as they hurried back to the village before they were missed for too long.

CHAPTER SEVEN
Mary

LEAH SHOULD HAVE REPRIMANDED THEM for delaying, Mary thought, but her sister-in-law was elated to have her husband home. She was also fussing over their guest, Horeb. The man had his donkey in a stall behind the house, although the donkey seemed too old to be a useful beast of burden.

Mary had nearly forgotten about Horeb and all that Lazarus had told her about wanting to share his experiences. The cries and screams of the little girl inside the tent had wrenched Mary's heart. She'd almost gone into the tent to see if she could help, but then the crying had stopped, and Martha had come out.

If there was one thing Mary knew for sure, it was that her sister was the strongest and bravest woman she knew. Martha never shirked her duties. She always put others first. She worked day and night to make life better for others. All of this only made Mary realize how selfish she'd been by keeping to her own world and imaginations. She needed to be a better sister and a better woman. She should not be complaining about the blessing of becoming Isaac's wife and mother to his children.

Like Zachary's little girl, Isaac's children were motherless. Who was Mary to resent such a gift to fulfill that role upon the day of her vows to a good man?

"Can you take this to our guest?" Leah asked, pointing to a tray of olives and clay cups of wine. "Once the refreshments are served, we can listen to what Lazarus has to say."

Since Mary had been with Martha, no one questioned their late arrival. Then as soon as they'd reached home, Martha had gone to greet Lazarus and meet Horeb. Mary had been hovering in the cooking room, not wanting to join the others yet.

Why? She wasn't sure. She'd never been particularly shy, but something about Horeb made her antsy.

Mary picked up the tray, and with Leah following behind her at a slower gait, Mary entered the gathering room. The area was a good size, strewn with cushions, rugs, and a low table in the center. Lazarus had entertained plenty of guests in this room, and it was Leah's pride and joy. She'd embroidered many of the cushions over the years, and they'd all worked on weaving the rugs.

Now Lazarus sat at the head of the table lounging on a cushion, his face all smiles as Mary walked in. She didn't look at Horeb, who sat fairly close to her, because his presence alone had already affected her. And the last thing she wanted was for Martha, or, heaven forbid, Lazarus, to notice her curiosity about their guest.

Rhode and Nathaniel held back no measure of their curiosity, and their eager faces were alert and attentive. Little Naomi snuggled against her father's side, and he kept an affectionate arm about his daughter.

It was good to see Naomi healed and back to her sweet self, eyes bright and cheeks full of color.

Mary settled next to Martha at the far end of the table, sitting carefully on a cushion so that she didn't take up more than her share of space. From her position, it was quite easy to take in a full view of Horeb. Perhaps she'd allow herself one deliberate glance, but then her attention needed to remain on her brother.

But instead of Lazarus starting out with a tale of his travels and trading business, he turned to Horeb and motioned with his cup. "You have all met Horeb, and first, I want to make an announcement. He will be staying with us and working for me. He has no family to speak of, at least until two days ago, when he became like a brother to me."

Mary stared at Lazarus. What in heaven's name had happened to make Horeb such an essential part of Lazarus's life?

Lazarus continued. "I don't want to do all the talking tonight, so Horeb will start from the beginning, for the tale I bring takes place well before I met this young man at an inn where he was trying to get his donkey to take but one step."

Horeb smiled, and the glance that took place between the two told Mary they were close friends indeed. Like brothers. But how?

"As you see, my donkey is in the twilight of his life," Horeb said. "But like me, he is a stubborn beast. Food and a couple days' rest at the inn was all he needed."

Mary marveled that the stubborn donkey had made it all the way to Bethany.

Horeb took a sip from his cup, then looked about the small family gathering. "First, I'd like to thank you for your hospitality. Lazarus has told me about his wife and children and of his two sisters, but I never imagined I would be blessed enough to visit your home and meet each of you. I have never been the recipient of such generosity, and I will surely spend every hour of every day trying to repay your kindness."

Leah smiled, and Martha nodded.

Mary looked down at her lap, where she'd primly folded her hands.

"When Lazarus asked me to return to Bethany with him and work in his grove, I thought I had been handed the greatest blessing of my life." Horeb paused. "Well, the second-greatest blessing."

At this, Mary looked up. What could he mean?

Horeb rose to his feet and lifted his tunic halfway up his calves.

Mary felt a blush heat her cheeks.

"I was born with a deformed foot," Horeb said, extending one of his legs. "I couldn't walk far without tiring. I needed a cane to do any work, and I was frequently without a way to buy food. Some had pity on me and would offer me a few days' labor in exchange for food. But I'd be sent away after a short time because I could not produce as much as a whole man."

He lowered his tunic and sat down. "Lazarus brought a miracle into my life. And like he said, he found me coaxing my donkey to move, but my donkey was in worse shape than I. But I was desperate, you see, to reach the Healer."

The healer must be a skilled physician indeed. Someone from Galilee, Mary assumed.

"For I knew the Master Healer could change my life, and He did because I am completely whole now," Horeb said. "None of it would have happened if Lazarus had not driven me in his cart to where Jesus was."

"Jesus? Is He this Master Healer you speak of?" Rhode asked.

Everyone in the room wanted to know the answer to that exact question. Horeb looked at Lazarus then.

Mary's brother nodded. "We traveled back to Galilee in search of Jesus. I didn't know why Horeb was so adamant about meeting the man. Horeb's conviction was so strong that this Jesus could heal him that I suppose I was curious. And then we met others traveling to see Jesus, and we ran across Sarah."

"A blind woman," Horeb said.

"Who now sees everything," Lazarus finished with a smile and a slight tremble to his tone.

"Jesus is not an ordinary man," Horeb continued. His voice was quiet, but it carried to every rapt listener. "He heals not with poultices or teas or bandages but with the power of God."

Mary could not take her eyes off Horeb. His countenance was bright, and his eyes were warm, full of conviction. Could his story be true? Had he been lame and now was fully healed? Her brother was a witness, it seemed, so Mary had to believe.

She glanced at her sister Martha, and their gazes connected briefly but significantly. A healer such as Jesus could heal a young girl like Claudia if He could make the blind see and the lame walk.

"But that's not all Jesus healed," Lazarus said. "Jesus can heal us spiritually and emotionally. He can ease our sorrows and comfort our broken hearts. He can forgive us for our sins. For He is the light of this world."

Mary stared at her brother. What did he mean? What was he saying? Only God could forgive.

Horeb folded his hands atop the table, glancing at each of the family members. "When I told Lazarus about Jesus, he didn't know what to think. He didn't believe, but he was willing to help me regardless. Lazarus is a good man—in fact, the best man that I know. Even Jesus saw that in him."

Lazarus released a breath. "I do not deserve your praise, Horeb. I owe you so much more than I could ever repay."

Mary looked from one man to the next.

Tears spilled onto her brother's cheeks, but he made no effort to brush them away. "I have called the family together so that I might testify that the prophesies of Isaiah have been fulfilled. 'For unto us a child is born, unto us a son is given: and the government shall be upon his shoulder: and his name shall be called Wonderful, Counsellor, The mighty God, The everlasting Father, The Prince of Peace.'"

Mary blinked back her own tears. She recognized the words her brother was quoting because she'd read Isaiah's prophecies for herself. Her father had been at her side, helping her sound out letters and words until she could read them on her own. She used her mantle to wipe at the moisture on her face.

"Husband," Leah whispered, her eyes wide and luminous with tears. "What are you saying?"

Lazarus turned his tearful gaze toward her. "I am saying, dear Leah, that I stood in the presence of the Messiah. I have met the Redeemer. I watched Him perform miracles that cannot be explained by man."

"He is in Galilee?" Martha whispered.

"Yes," Horeb confirmed. "He travels from town to town with His Apostles, bringing good news and the message of salvation to all."

Mary gazed openly at Horeb. There was a light about this man she'd never witnessed before in a person, and she realized it was because he was without judgment or worldly concern. She also sensed he was trustworthy and honest.

Horeb's mouth curved into a soft smile. "Your brother told me you are a learned woman, Mary. Surely you know of the prophecies of old."

"Yes," Mary whispered.

"Then you know the prophecy about His mother?"

Mary swallowed. "'Therefore the Lord himself shall give you a sign; Behold, a virgin shall conceive, and bear a son, and shall call his name Immanuel.'"

Horeb's smile seemed to light the entire room. "Yes," he said with shining eyes. "Jesus has been born of Mary of Nazareth, a virgin."

Many times Mary had wondered how such a thing was possible, for a virgin to conceive, but she had never questioned it openly before.

It seemed Horeb understood her curiosity. "Mary of Nazareth was overcome by the Holy Spirit and conceived the Messiah. She is of the lineage of David, and when she was with child, she traveled with her new husband, Joseph, to the land of her ancestors: Bethlehem. She gave birth to her son there."

Warmth flashed across her skin at the realization that this was another prophecy, this one by the prophet Micah.

Lazarus cleared his throat. "Micah said, 'But thou, Beth-lehem Ephratah, though thou be little among the thousands of Judah, yet out of thee shall he come forth unto me that is to be ruler in Israel; whose goings forth have been from of old, from everlasting.'"

Horeb nodded, and Mary used her mantle to wipe at new tears.

"Family," Lazarus continued, "we must prepare to receive the Messiah not only in our hearts but also in our home."

"Jesus is coming to Bethany?" Leah asked in a stunned tone.

"To our home?" Martha added.

The Messiah was coming to Bethany . . . Mary couldn't wrap her mind around it. She grabbed for Martha's hand, and her sister held on tight. Mary could ask Jesus her questions. Would she ever see her parents again? Would she be a good wife to Isaac? Could she be a mother to children who were not of her own flesh? Surely the Messiah would know the answers, but were they too petty for Him?

Lazarus continued to tell how he and Horeb had waited to see Jesus because there were hundreds of others who'd flocked to meet Him, how that number had grown to the thousands and Jesus had continued performing miracle after miracle.

"He fed four thousand people with a few fishes and loaves," Lazarus said.

"How?" Nathaniel piped up. Both he and Rhode had been silent for the most part.

"That is the miracle," Horeb said. "The baskets that were passed around with the fishes and loaves never became empty, no matter how many were taken out."

An hour passed, then two, but everyone was completely absorbed in the stories of Jesus. Eventually Naomi fell asleep in her mother's arms, and at one point, Martha went to fetch more refreshments. Mary didn't want to miss one word, and a wild beast couldn't have dragged her away.

Horeb told of the unclean spirits Jesus had cast out, the lepers He'd cleansed, the infants He'd healed, the palsy He'd cured. Horeb told of the Apostles, men who ministered to others in the crowd, and although Mary knew she wouldn't be able to recall all of their names, she was fascinated.

And then she remembered. In all her study and learning, she'd also read about how the Messiah would be rejected by His own people and then betrayed by one of His followers. Would that be an Apostle? She wanted to ask her questions, but she didn't want to interrupt. Did the Messiah know about the prophecies about His life and His . . . death? Did he know Isaiah had prophesied that He would be tried and condemned? That He would be accused and oppressed and led like a lamb to the slaughter?

The tears that came now were not ones of wonder and astonishment but of grief for a man she'd never met. One who was innocent in all things yet who would be smitten and spat upon, mocked and taunted, and then finally led to His death to suffer among the sinners.

"Mary, why are you crying?" Martha whispered, wrapping an arm about her.

She was crying; she was quietly sobbing, and she couldn't stop. She didn't know what had come over her, but she couldn't stop thinking of an innocent, loving man, like her father, like her brother, and even like Horeb, undergoing such horrific treatment. As if it made sense in any mind to punish and put to death a man who spent His days serving and healing others. Healing hearts, minds, and bodies.

"Come," Martha said. "Let's go get more refreshment, and you'll have a chance to calm yourself."

"All right." Mary's voice was small and her eyes too blurry to see as she rose from her cushion and walked with Martha into the cooking room.

CHAPTER EIGHT
Martha

MARTHA HAD NOT READ THE scrolls that her sister had, nor had she studied the words of the ancient prophets so in depth. But she was familiar enough with the elders' teachings and knew that the coming of the Messiah was significant indeed.

But right now, her sister was inconsolable, and Martha needed to give her a respite. Whatever troubled her so deeply, she'd find out soon enough.

"Let's step outside and get some fresh air," Martha said, guiding Mary into the back courtyard.

Mary nodded, wiping at her face with her mantle—a mantle that would almost need to be wrung out and hung to dry with all of those tears she was mopping up.

"Are you all right?" Martha asked, grasping her sister's shoulders.

Mary sniffled. "Do you not understand? The prophecies speak of the birth of the Messiah, but they also speak of His death."

Martha furrowed her brow. Of course she knew this . . . perhaps. She hadn't dwelt on it, though, not as Mary apparently had.

"Micah and Isaiah both prophesied that the Messiah would be smitten and spat upon," Mary said. "And that's not all. He will be wounded for our transgressions and bruised for our iniquities."

The words were familiar, and Martha remembered that there was more that they'd learned. She exhaled. "Yes, so that we are healed and forgiven."

Mary blinked as if she had been too focused on the devastation instead of the outcome.

"Remember what our brother and Horeb said?" Martha added. "The Messiah is here to spread the *good* news. He is here to redeem us and bring salvation unto all men."

Mary bit her trembling lip. "What about those who are not alive to hear His message? Mother and Father? What about Yosef?"

Martha's eyes widened at the mention of Yosef. She'd kept her sorrow and grief silent for the most part. But she didn't feel offended or hurt; instead, she gave a soft smile. "Perhaps we can ask the Messiah Himself when He comes to Bethany."

"Do you really think He'll come?" Mary whispered, even though there was no one about to hear them. "To our small village?"

"We can only hope," Martha said in a rush. "And we will have much to prepare."

"Yes." Mary nodded. "Can you imagine what it will be like seeing His face? Being in His presence? A man so powerful, a man who is the very Messiah." Her voice stopped, and she wiped at her cheeks again.

Martha could not stand by and watch her sister cry, so she pulled her into her arms for a long moment. When Mary's shudders passed, Martha said, "Can you come with me to see Zachary and Claudia again?"

Mary drew away and gave a watery smile. "I can. Our brother and his guest have enough refreshments, and we will return in time to help Leah with supper preparations."

Martha smiled in return. "That is what I was thinking."

The two sisters hurried out of the courtyard together. The sun was still high in the sky, but they kept to the back roads so as not to encounter anyone if possible. Despite all that had been said at home about Jesus of Nazareth, her thoughts had continually strayed toward the little girl suffering in a shepherd's tent. If the Messiah were here, would He visit Claudia? Martha wanted to believe He would.

They made good time to the fields, and all was quiet when they approached the tent. "At least she's not crying anymore," Mary said.

Yes, it was a relief, Martha thought as she remembered the heart-wrenching sounds from their earlier visit. She stepped up to the tent and called out in a soft voice, not wanting to disturb Claudia's slumber quite yet. "Zachary? It's Martha. I've returned with Mary."

No one answered, and there was no sound within the tent. "Zachary?" Martha tried again. Mary's clear worry mirrored her own.

What if something had happened to Claudia, and Zachary had taken her somewhere?

"We should go in," Mary suggested in a timid voice that was unlike her.

"All right." Martha pushed aside the tent flap.

Mary followed. The interior of the tent was warmer than the outside winter air but not as warm as their home. It took only seconds for Martha to understand why Zachary hadn't answered her quiet call. He lay on his side next to his daughter. One of his hands clasped hers, and they were both sound asleep.

Martha watched for a moment as Zachary's chest rose and fell with slumber. The hollows below his eyes were still visible, but the lines about his face were relaxed, and his forehead seemed worry-free. She hated to wake him, but his daughter needed attention.

Her eyes flicked to the basket she'd brought earlier that day—still on the table—and she quietly walked over to it and pulled out another herbal root. Mary joined her at the table. "Can you stoke the outside fire and warm up water for tea?"

Mary took the root without a word and followed where Martha pointed to the opening in the tent that connected to the cooking fire.

Martha approached the sleeping pair and knelt next to Claudia. She gazed at her sweet face for a moment, and then she looked at how Zachary enclosed his daughter's hand. It was something Martha had never had in her life—a child—and now she had no husband to care for a child anyway.

She tucked away the sting of emotion that always seemed to take over at unexpected times and placed a hand on Claudia's forehead. Her skin was cool to the touch, and her slumber remained deep.

Zachary suddenly shifted and opened his eyes, his attention landing on her. Martha withdrew her hand.

"You're here," Zachary rasped, lines carving his forehead. "I didn't mean to fall asleep."

"I'm sorry I let myself in," Martha whispered quickly. "My sister is preparing more tea."

Zachary pushed up on an elbow, then sat up. They were still close, only Claudia separating them, and the tent suddenly felt much smaller than it already was. Zachary ran his fingers through his dark hair, which was more unruly than she'd seen it earlier. Then his gaze flicked to where Mary was working just outside the tent. When his eyes locked with Martha's again, he said, "I have good news."

This surprised her. "Oh?"

"I fed Claudia the rest of the tea, and she drank most of it," he said. "She didn't say one word about a lion."

"Wonderful," Martha said, her chest expanding. She couldn't help but smile, and Zachary smiled back. Seeing Zachary smile, truly smile, did something odd to Martha's belly—making it feel warm and light and fluttery.

She quickly looked down before something else could happen, like her cheeks heating with a blush. She focused on the sleeping child. "Her color looks better."

"I'm grateful for you, Martha," Zachary said.

She couldn't look at him, not now, not when she was sure his attention was on her. Not when her cheeks were threatening to bloom like a red rose. "I am just happy she's doing better."

"You came unbidden," Zachary continued, his tone low. Perhaps so Mary couldn't hear? Or so that his daughter would keep sleeping? "Josiah couldn't help me. The village healer was afraid to touch her because he claimed an unclean spirit dwelt within."

Martha nodded. She knew all of this yet let him say it again. It was as if he were rambling, or perhaps this was how he sorted through his thoughts.

"I haven't always been a desperate shepherd living in a small tent," he said.

This caught her attention, and she looked up then, into his dark-brown eyes. She found herself wondering how he'd gotten the scar just above his lip and if he'd been born with the slight crook at the top of his nose. She also wondered how old he was. Older than she was, she guessed. Perhaps in his thirtieth year?

"My brother and I . . . we didn't see eye to eye," Zachary said. "He was married to a woman who claimed she had loved me first. And my wife had had enough of her insinuations. My wife miscarried three times after Claudia. She said it was because of the hatred in the home we shared with my brother. She said that an innocent babe couldn't thrive amongst such vileness. So we decided to leave Jerusalem forever. To leave all the bad blood, backbiting, ill will, and jealousy behind."

Martha stared, then blinked. She had no words. This was not what she expected to hear at all.

"But then . . ." He dropped his eyes and smoothed back his daughter's hair. "She became with child here in Bethany. Finally, it was a new beginning. I hadn't seen her so happy in years." His voice broke.

Martha's heart cracked because she knew the outcome of that happiness. She wanted to reach a hand out to him, place her fingers on his forearm. She knew grief well. But she didn't move, didn't touch him. "I'm sorry about your wife and babe, Zachary."

Tears dripped onto his cheeks, and he quickly brushed them away, blinked hard, then nodded.

"Some say it was God's will," he whispered, his voice imprinted with pain. "But how can God take a beautiful woman and an innocent child?"

Martha's own eyes stung with tears. This was a question she'd asked over and over and never found an answer for. "I don't know." It was perhaps the most honest answer she could give. Perhaps . . . perhaps the Messiah Himself would have the answer.

But she couldn't very well speak of that right now—not when it wasn't her story to tell. "I think you should talk to my brother. He's a wise man."

Before Zachary could respond, Mary brought the hot water inside, and Martha rose to help her at the table. It was good to have a little distance from Zachary. His confessions, exposing the deep parts of his heart, had shaken Martha and had made her remember her own deeply buried grief over expectations lost.

She and Yosef weren't in love, not at first. They'd been a good match, though, compatible, and once, when Yosef became ill, Martha had spent day and night caring for him. Washing, feeding, comforting . . . it was then that she'd realized she did, indeed, love Yosef. Through serving him when he was at his most vulnerable, her heart had awakened. Her only regret was not telling him before he went on that final journey.

She had told him, though. Over and over. To his closed eyes and lifeless form when his shrouded body had been brought to her home for a final farewell. Her greatest and only gift in return was when Lazarus had shared something Yosef had told him on their journey.

"I have fallen in love with my wife," Yosef had told Lazarus. "It will be the first thing I tell her when I see her again."

He had died, though, and had never spoken the words to her.

But they had been spoken—to her brother—and she would never forget that.

"Martha?" Mary said.

Martha focused on her sister, wondering how many times her name had been called.

"Do you want help with Claudia?"

"I-I think Zachary and I can manage it," Martha said, taking the clay cup of tea and joining Zachary at his daughter's side again.

Martha nodded to him, but instead of nodding back, his gaze held hers. And she knew, somehow she knew he would understand the grief she'd experienced. For his was the same.

Then he broke the connection and moved to the top of the mat, gently pulling Claudia into his arms.

Her eyes opened, fluttering for a moment, then opened wider, her brow pinched at the sight of Martha.

"Hello, Claudia," Martha said in a soft tone. "I have some tea for you to drink. It's warm, and it will help you get better."

Claudia said nothing but glanced up at her father, who nodded. "Drink the tea."

Obediently, Claudia opened her mouth. It was a much different experience than the last time, and Martha held the cup as the girl sipped down the liquid.

When Claudia finished, her eyes tracked across the tent. "Who's that?"

"Mary, my sister," Martha said, thrilled that there didn't seem to be any lions lurking in the tent but that Claudia was indeed seeing reality.

"She's pretty."

Martha smiled. "She is pretty." When Zachary's gaze shifted to Mary as well, Martha's stomach did a slow turn.

What did he think of her sister? She was unmarried, about to be betrothed, but there was no doubt she was the beautiful sister in their family.

Mary clasped her hands in front of her, her movements feminine and dainty. Something that Martha had rarely paid attention to. Everything Mary did was graceful. "How are you feeling, Claudia?" Mary asked.

Claudia's mouth curved. "Better. The lion is gone."

So she remembered her hallucination.

Martha couldn't help but grasp the girl's hand. The girl's recovery was more important than the fact that Zachary had more than noticed Mary. "I'm so glad to hear that," Martha said. "Are you feeling hungry yet?"

Claudia nodded, and Martha smiled. "Wonderful. I'll make something for you to eat."

As she rose to her feet, she glanced at Zachary. His focus was on her, not Mary. For some reason, this fact alone brought heat to her cheeks. She turned away and moved toward the table. Quickly, she prepared a broth, and then, in the next moment, she was back at Claudia's side.

The little girl was mostly sitting up, still leaning against her father, and he'd made no move to release her.

It was endearing, truthfully.

Martha lifted a spoonful of the broth to Claudia's lips, and she dutifully swallowed it down.

"I can sit up now and feed myself," Claudia said, shifting forward, away from her father.

"Good girl," Zachary murmured. Then he rose to his feet, his head nearly touching the top of the tent.

Martha remained next to Claudia, holding the bowl of broth, while the girl took a few bites.

"You are hungry," Martha said. "How is your stomach?"

Claudia shrugged. "All right. I'm tired, though."

"I'll bet you are," Martha said. "Maybe another bite, and then we'll let you sleep."

As Claudia obediently ate, Mary fetched a cloth from the basket and wetted it, then knelt next to the girl. "Would you like me to wash your hands and face?"

Claudia held out her hands, and Mary worked to clean the young girl's hands and face. They'd been grimy, Martha realized now, but she had been focused on other things.

"Can you comb my hair?" Claudia whispered to Martha. "My mother used to do that."

Martha's gaze slipped to Zachary, who was standing, his hands on his hips as he watched the scene. She saw the flash of pain in his eyes, but he cleared his throat and said, "I'll get the comb."

"I'd be happy to comb your hair." Martha tamped down the burst of pride that swept through her at being chosen for the task. It was nothing, really. She'd combed Naomi's hair many times, so at least she was skilled at being gentle.

After a moment, Zachary brought over a comb, and Martha shifted closer to Claudia, then began to comb through the tangled strands. Martha started at the bottom, then worked her way upward. Zachary moved about the tent, seeming restless as he shifted things around, folded a couple of rugs, stepped outside, then came back in.

Mary simply sat on one of the cushions, her expression contemplative.

When Martha finished combing Claudia's hair, she began to plait it.

"Who are your friends?" Mary asked.

Claudia shrugged her thin shoulders. "The sheep."

Martha wanted to laugh, but she didn't.

"You should come play with our niece, Naomi," Mary said. "She's younger than you, but she'd love to have someone to look up to."

Claudia's smile peeked out again. "What would we do?"

Martha hid a frown. Had this girl never had a playmate before?

"I could teach you embroidery," Mary suggested. "Or we can play with the baby goats."

"All right," Claudia said, her eyes brighter than they had been all day.

Martha was impressed with Mary's suggestion, and she wondered if Zachary would be too. He had called his wife beautiful, and Mary was certainly beautiful too.

CHAPTER NINE
Lazarus

"I CAN FETCH HER," LEAH told Lazarus well before dawn as he climbed out of bed at the sound of Naomi crying.

"You've enough to do," he said. "And you need rest for the child you are carrying." His wife was a capable woman, but Lazarus had seen the exhaustion streaked across her face over the past day he'd been home.

He was pleased that his sisters had taken most of the burdens from her, but Naomi would have to be satisfied with her father's comfort this morning. She'd been ill, and Lazarus was grateful she was on the mend, but it still worried him.

Many children in their village had been ill, and last night, news had reached him that a young girl—the daughter of a shepherd—was at death's door. Zachary was the shepherd's name. Lazarus had seen the man at synagogue but had never had a conversation with him.

Now Lazarus entered the adjoining bedchamber where Naomi was sitting on her bed mat, crying. She was old enough to find her way to her parents' sleeping place, but since her illness, she expected her mother to come to her.

"Naomi," Lazarus whispered. "What is wrong?" He drew her small body into his arms, and she immediately clung to him.

"I want Mother."

"She's sleeping," Lazarus said. "Remember she has to rest for the babe."

"My sister?"

"Brother or sister," Lazarus clarified, although the gender of the child was no matter to him. God had already blessed him with two healthy sons. Lazarus rubbed a hand over his daughter's back, hoping to soothe her to sleep. Previous experience had taught him that a tired Naomi was an irritable Naomi.

"Father," Naomi said, her voice tiny in the near darkness. "Does Horeb have a family?"

"Not anymore," Lazarus said. "We are his family now."

And it was true. Lazarus had felt a bond with Horeb he couldn't explain. The experiences they'd gone through together, learning at Jesus's feet as He taught the four thousand about becoming like little children, had made Lazarus realize that kindness and service to his fellow men would never be paralleled. Jesus's words echoed in his mind: "Whosoever therefore shall humble himself as this little child, the same is greatest in the kingdom of heaven."

There was no reason Lazarus shouldn't help Horeb. Yes, Lazarus already had laborers he paid, but there had been several years of plenty, and Horeb was eager to work and prove his new physical capabilities.

Lazarus realized he was humming and his heart was full, and as the moments passed, Naomi relaxed farther into his arms. Soon, she fell asleep, and he carefully shifted her onto the bed again. He drew a rug around her, then gazed at her small features in the soft, gray light of the approaching dawn.

All of his children were precious to him, but something about his daughter truly tugged at his heart. Her excitement for the small things in life, how she threw her arms about his neck whenever he stepped into the house, and how she giggled without restraint. She was a delight.

Lazarus crept out of the bedchamber, careful to not make a sound. He was blessed, more than blessed. The three-story house held room for everyone, including Horeb. Martha and Mary agreed to share the upper floor, yet Horeb had insisted on sleeping outside, although Leah had tried to talk him into at least putting a mat by the cooking-room hearth. He said he would keep an eye on his donkey, which had recovered fully and could soon be put to work.

Lazarus returned to his bedchamber to find that Leah was still awake. He crossed to her side of the bed and bent down to kiss her forehead. "She's gone back to sleep," he said. "You can as well."

Leah extended her arms, and Lazarus sat on the edge of the platform bed, then pulled her into an embrace. He breathed in her warm, honey-scented skin. He had missed his wife during his travels.

"Thank you, husband. You are too good to me."

He lifted his face from the silkiness of her hair. "You are too good to *me*, wife."

She smiled. It was something they said to each other often. Something just between them.

"I am going to walk to the groves, so don't trouble yourself about a morning meal for me or Horeb," he said. "We'll grab bread and goat cheese. I want to start teaching him how to inspect the trees. The sooner he learns the trade, the better."

Before he could pull away, Leah put a hand on Lazarus's arm. "Can you speak with Mary when you return?"

Lazarus frowned at the worry in his wife's voice. "Of course. Is there something the matter?"

"I am not sure," Leah said, rising to a sitting position with some effort. This brought her eye to eye with him. "Before you returned home, she had a discussion with Isaac, and I could tell it upset her. She didn't reveal a word to me, but she was very anxious for your return after that. I think she wants your counsel."

Lazarus's frown remained. "Did they argue?"

"I could not hear, but when he left, she wiped at tears in her eyes."

This Lazarus didn't like to hear. Relationships and marriage were complicated, but he worried that Mary's headstrong personality might be a deterrent even to the best of men. Still, Isaac had not visited Lazarus last night, so he considered that at least a good sign.

"There is more," Leah said. "She was entranced by Horeb."

"What do you mean?" Lazarus asked, hoping she didn't mean what she'd implied. "Horeb is young, and he's starting a new life."

"Horeb is a listener, and he is full of energy and light," Leah said, slipping her hand into his and interlocking their fingers. "He's like a warm breeze on a spring day, carrying with it the scent of flowers and honey."

With his other hand, Lazarus touched her jaw. "You are a poet, dear Leah."

Her expression softened, but concern was still etched in the faint lines of her face. "Mary is a dreamer. Her thoughts are not always focused on what is going on around her. She's often thinking of what she's been reading instead of her task at hand."

That was one way to put it. His two sisters were opposites in many ways. Martha was more like Leah and rarely rested or took time for herself. Mary was . . . inquisitive and curious, and her mind never seemed to tire of learning and asking questions.

"I will speak with her when I return from the grove," he said. "What time is the banquet tonight? I want to be sure I help where I can."

"Sundown," Leah said. "Our usual mealtime. Isaac's mother will be coming over earlier in the afternoon, most likely with his children, to help. Although I'm afraid they will only be underfoot."

Lazarus kissed his wife's forehead. "You are a marvel. I'd better get going so I can be home that much sooner."

Her smile was soft, and he wished today was not so full of tasks. He'd like nothing better than to slide beneath the covers, pull her into his arms, and doze until the sun made sleep impossible.

"Go, husband." Leah nudged him away. "I will be counting the minutes until your return."

He flashed her a smile, then quickly changed into clothing he wouldn't mind getting dusty. Later, he'd dress in a finer tunic and robe for their guests.

Horeb was nowhere to be seen in the cooking room, not that Lazarus was surprised. The young man had camped his way across the fields and valleys to make it to Galilee in the first place. When Lazarus opened the door to the back courtyard, wondering if he'd have to wake Horeb, he found him repairing the goat pen.

"What are you doing?" Lazarus asked as he approached.

"Did you know the gate is loose?" Horeb said. "This little one was butting it all night, and the rattling kept me awake."

"I'm very sorry," Lazarus said, crouching beside Horeb. The goat in question was now sound asleep. Apparently his all-night antics had worn him out.

"I waited until I could see something before I searched around the stable for tools." Horeb brushed his hands and straightened. "There. No more rattling, and no chance of escape."

"Thank you," Lazarus said. "But are you now too sleep-deprived to visit the grove with me?"

"I am fine." Horeb stifled a yawn, then chuckled. "I mean, my mind would not shut off anyway, then the goat began its antics. I'll sleep early tonight, perhaps, but a missed night of sleep has never harmed me. Especially when today is my first day of full-time employment."

Lazarus clapped a hand on Horeb's shoulder. "You're a remarkable young man. Follow me. Leah is already anxious for our return this afternoon. We're expecting a houseful of guests tonight for a banquet. Everyone will be interested in meeting you as well."

"Oh?" Horeb said. He motioned to the stall with his donkey in it. "I'm offering my donkey's services to anyone in your family. It's because of you he's alive today."

Lazarus chuckled. "I will tell them. Come on, my friend. We have a busy day ahead."

Horeb grinned and fell into step next to Lazarus, his bare feet padding along the ground.

Lazarus needed to get the young man some sandals. Soon. When he'd tried to purchase him something in Galilee, Horeb refused additional hospitality. But now that Horeb was his employee, perhaps he'd relent.

"It's Mary's betrothal banquet," Lazarus said.

"That's right," Horeb said. "You told me about that earlier, but I had no idea I'd be included."

Lazarus glanced at Horeb, thinking of what Leah had implied about Mary's interest in the young man. Surely it was only curiosity. Besides, Horeb didn't seem to have any special interest in Mary or Martha. He'd been eager to share his life story, surely, and how he was healed, but Horeb was young and had a few years before he needed to make life decisions, such as marriage.

They walked in silence for a few moments. The morning air was brisk, but it felt invigorating to walk through the quiet streets. It would be hours yet before the markets would come alive and the villagers would start their day. They passed houses and huts in the growing light with the deeper gray of the sky softening to a dusty violet.

"How old are you, Horeb?"

At this, Horeb shot him a wry glance. "I'm not entirely sure."

Lazarus's brows popped up at this. "What? Did your mother not tell you?"

"She was a mute, and communication was difficult."

Lazarus stopped walking and simply stared at his new friend. "You didn't share this information before."

Horeb's expression remained passive. "I suppose I didn't feel it necessary."

"Regardless," Lazarus said as they both started walking again. "How old do you think you are?"

"I would estimate twenty-four."

"You seem younger," Lazarus commented, realizing he wanted Horeb to be younger. Too young to take upon himself the responsibilities of a wife.

"I might seem younger because I've spent most of my life hiding or begging." Horeb lifted an arm and pinched his skin. "I've yet to be strong as a man, but I plan to fix that by working for you."

Lazarus chuckled. That was not why Horeb seemed young, although he was underweight. Horeb had a childlike innocence about him and a wonder-filled expression when he talked of things he was passionate about—like Jesus of Nazareth. Horeb wasn't jaded or bitter or angry . . . as he had every right to be, considering the hard lot he'd been dealt in life.

Did anger and bitterness make a man age? Lazarus had never reflected on that possibility, but he guessed it to be true.

"Your sisters are remarkable women," Horeb said suddenly. "I can tell there is a lot of love and harmony in your home, and the children benefit."

Lazarus looked at Horeb. "They are not perfect, and there are plenty of disagreements."

Horeb smiled. "I've no doubt, but love is the foundation, which is what matters. They will stick together as family should. Something I hope to have someday."

Lazarus couldn't help but pry. "What do you hope for in your future, Horeb?"

"I've already got everything I could hope for," he said with a smile. "My foot is healed, I am employed, and I have a new friend."

"Great, then I can put you to work, my friend."

Horeb chuckled, and Lazarus found himself grinning despite the early hour of the morning and the stretch of work before him. The only wrinkle was what Mary wanted to speak with him about.

Otherwise, the next few hours passed quickly as Lazarus walked the grove with Horeb and taught him about his cultivation methods. They also checked on the wheat and barley Lazarus had planted between the trees while the olive production was dormant. When the laborers showed up, Lazarus introduced Horeb to them. Horeb was cheerful and seemed to get along with everyone he met.

The afternoon was wearing on when, finally, Lazarus had done what he'd set out to do. He'd return tomorrow and make it an extra productive day. "Come, Horeb," Lazarus said. "We'll return home and share in Leah's work."

Horeb turned from watering the rows of crops with his wooden bucket. "All right."

"And perhaps eat."

"That would be nice."

Lazarus chuckled. His own stomach had been grumbling for a good two hours. But as they reached the edge of the grove that joined up with the main village road, Lazarus was surprised to see Isaac approaching.

Isaac was older than Lazarus by a few years and had always done well as one of the main farmers in Bethany. He rotated wheat, barley, and grains, such as lentils and peas. But he and Lazarus had never been close friends, even though they weren't exactly competitors.

"Your family told me you'd returned and I could find you here," Isaac said by way of greeting. His observant gaze cut to Horeb, and Lazarus introduced the two men.

They were opposites in demeanor and personality. Horeb's easy laughter and cheerfulness contrasted with Isaac's more somber personality.

"I did not expect to see you until tonight," Lazarus said.

Isaac folded his arms. "I wanted to speak to you before the betrothal ceremony and not around the others."

"I can wait over here," Horeb said without being asked. He moved off and found a spot to sit on the low wall that edged the road.

Lazarus looked back at Isaac, the man who was soon to be his brother-in-law.

"Certain activities that Mary is involved in have come to my attention," Isaac began without any preamble.

If Isaac had punched Lazarus in the stomach, he couldn't have been more surprised. Surely, if anything nefarious had happened, Leah or Martha would have told him.

"What is going on, Isaac?" Lazarus asked, his eagerness to get home having all but faded.

"You very well know that Mary spends her free time reading scrolls and texts that are not of her concern," Isaac said.

Lazarus opened his mouth to protest, but Isaac pressed on, his tone firm.

"My mother told me she's seen her outside the synagogue a handful of times."

"Yes," Lazarus cut in, not liking where this was going. "She takes the midday meal to my sons so they can continue their studies during the break."

Isaac's brow only wrinkled farther. "She arrives much too early for the meal break. My mother says Mary . . . lingers. And she asks many questions of your sons on the way home."

Lazarus had no idea how Isaac could know this, but it was a strange thing to be bothered about. Why was Isaac concerned over conversation among family members? Yes, Mary was inquisitive, but that was no sin.

"Mary finds value in many things in life," Lazarus finally answered, since it seemed that an answer was required. "Including understanding the psalms, the laws, and the prophets' teachings."

Isaac moved closer and lowered his voice. "You need to speak to her and explain that marriage brings heavy responsibility and increased expectations."

Lazarus's neck burned. "She understands that very well."

But the expression on Isaac's face told Lazarus he wasn't entirely believed.

Isaac folded his arms, his steely eyes narrowed. "I will not have a wife who gives cause for gossip."

Lazarus's restrained annoyance burst forth like a scavenging bird. "The only gossip I hear is coming from *you*, Isaac."

The man visibly flinched, but Lazarus didn't break eye contact. Not until Isaac broke it first as he turned and strode away, muttering under his breath.

Although Horeb had given their conversation privacy, Lazarus was sure the young man hadn't missed much.

The two of them headed into the village, silence a wedge between them. Lazarus knew he had to speak to Mary before the ceremony. This must be what Leah had referred to. Surely, Isaac was just reacting to his mother's observations. One couldn't be busy at tasks every minute of the day. Even with children in the household, Mary would have stolen moments to read. Lazarus had always been impressed with what his youngest sister could glean from her studies. He couldn't imagine a Mary without her scrolls and questions.

"Mary is young," Horeb said.

Lazarus was so caught up in his thoughts that he'd nearly forgotten he had a traveling companion. He glanced at Horeb, whose expression was open yet thoughtful.

"She is past the typical marrying age for our village," Lazarus said, "and her youth is well-nigh gone."

Horeb kicked a pebble out of the way. "Would you be upset if your wife wanted to spend time each day studying?"

"No," Lazarus said immediately. "I mean, I haven't thought of it that way, but I would be happy if Leah took a rest every now and then to do what she loved. Whether it was studying or something else."

"And Mary loves reading and learning of things beyond household duties," Horeb clarified.

"Yes."

"Why would a husband want to take away his wife's pleasure?"

Lazarus had no answer, and perhaps that troubled him most. "It's true that Mary is not the typical woman," he said at last. "She did not socialize with the other young women her age, and she avoided festivals in favor of a quiet night at home reading. My father had begun to discuss betrothal arrangements just before he passed away. After our mourning period, Isaac was the first to offer. In a small village like Bethany, time and selection aren't widely available."

Horeb said nothing to this, and once again, Lazarus was soon caught up in his own thoughts about how he was going to have a discussion with Mary.

CHAPTER TEN

Martha

ALMOST EVERY SURFACE OF THE cooking room was covered with trays of food, and the guests would begin arriving at any moment. But Martha wasn't bustling about, making sure everything was in order. No, she stood outside Mary's bedchamber door while she and Lazarus spoke. Well, Lazarus was speaking, and Mary was crying.

Martha sighed.

She hadn't meant to eavesdrop, but she'd come upstairs to see if Mary needed help getting ready. Martha hadn't realized that her brother was having a private conversation with her, but before she could return to the cooking room, Mary's words coming through the closed door had given her pause.

"Isaac cannot expect me to forget everything I've learned and be imprisoned in his home," Mary had said.

"That is not what he means," Lazarus had replied. "He only expects you to put aside that which is not necessary."

And that's when Mary started crying. "But it *is* necessary. To me."

Martha should have left the pair to their conversation, but her feet stayed rooted to the spot as Mary told Lazarus all that Isaac had said to her earlier in the day. Lazarus then confirmed the same things, having had his own conversation with the man.

"I understand your feelings, Mary," Lazarus said. "Life is challenging for us. You will have a husband, though, and that is a blessing. You will someday have your own children, and they will bring you much joy. Isaac's children also need a mother, and you are doing them a great and noble service."

"I know all of that," Mary said, her voice breaking. "So why am I afraid to make a commitment? It's like I don't know my own mind. I am questioning all I have believed in my future with Isaac."

"If you can't trust your own thoughts right now, then trust me," Lazarus said. "Do you think I'd allow you to marry a man who would mistreat you? Isaac is kind and generous. He can provide for you as a wife and for any future children. Your sons will inherit portions of his lands. And yes, he has expectations, but so would any husband."

The silence stretched inside the room.

"I don't know, Lazarus," Mary said at last. "Maybe I'm not meant for marriage and children."

Mary was upset and emotional; that much was clear. Was it her nerves or something more making her speak this way? Martha could no longer stand by, and she cracked open the door.

Her brother and sister both looked over, Mary's face tearstained, Lazarus's expression one of frustrated patience.

"Can I help?" Martha asked in a quiet voice.

Mary clutched her robe closer and turned away.

Lazarus sighed, then crossed the room and placed a hand on Martha's shoulder. "I hope you can help. I need to go downstairs to welcome our guests. They'll arrive at any moment."

Martha nodded and watched Lazarus slip out of the room. Then she turned toward her sister. Mary had moved to the window and was staring out at the fading light of day. Slowly, Martha approached her sister. Without touching her or facing her, Martha looked out the window too.

Beyond their property, the hills of Bethany rolled like a rippling silk cloth, hugging the base of the Mount of Olives. Their usual green color had been scrubbed pale by the winter upon them. Past the hills and homes, the patchy fields stretched, then disappeared into the deepening twilight.

"What is your greatest fear, Mary?" Martha asked after a few moments.

Mary sniffled. "That I won't be loved."

Martha snapped her head to gaze at her sister. "You are loved greatly by your entire family. And surely Isaac cares for you, or he would not have offered to take you as his wife."

Mary blinked her watery eyes. "I'm leaving this house, Martha. I'm leaving all that I know and love. Who will love me at Isaac's?"

"Isaac will love you in time," Martha said, touching her sister's arm. "His mother and children will grow to love you soon enough."

Mary's gaze dropped, and when she next lifted her tearful brown eyes, she whispered, "What if I'm miserable because I miss all of you?"

"Oh, Mary," Martha said. "We aren't going anywhere. We'll see each other every day, and our families will share frequent meals together like we do with Leah's. Bethany is a small village, you know."

"I know."

Martha squeezed her sister's arm. "Happiness is for you to create. Be a kind and obedient wife. Care for his children and respect his mother. In turn, you will be revered."

Mary's breath came out stuttered. "Is it so easy?"

"I will pray for you every day."

A small smile edged Mary's mouth. "Can you pray twice a day?"

Martha laughed, then pulled Mary into an embrace, but the laughter also brought tears with it, for Martha would miss her sister too, and the challenges would be great for Mary.

Voices rose from the floor below—a deeper voice that could only be Isaac's and other voices that must include the other invited guests.

Mary drew back and wiped at her eyes, then took a courageous breath. "I'll be down straightaway. I must change my robe. This one is wrinkled and damp from all my fretting."

Martha nodded, then stepped away from her sister. She gave her a gentle smile before leaving the bedchamber. Downstairs, the guests were already being directed to sit on pillows and pads. Isaac was the guest of honor, of course, and others had arrived with him—siblings and cousins.

His mother, Delilah, was in the cooking room with Leah, examining every dish with her sharp gaze. Martha didn't know Delilah well, but the woman had a reputation for not being the forgiving sort. Leah's face was flushed, and Martha was pretty sure it wasn't from the heat of the cooking fire.

"How long did you bake these honey cakes?" Delilah asked Leah. "They don't look quite right."

Before Leah could respond, Martha cut in. "I pulled them out before they could brown all the way because they continue to cook for a few moments after. I think you'll enjoy them just the same."

"I love honey cakes," Naomi announced. She was sitting near the hearth, wrapped in a rug. Her coloring was back to normal, but Leah had still restricted her from general activity.

"How old are *you*, Naomi?" Delilah asked.

Naomi held up four fingers.

"I see." Delilah gave a curt nod. "Old enough to help the rest of us."

"She's been ill like many of the other children in the village," Leah explained.

Delilah turned her gaze on Leah. "Children need routine night and day. That is how they stay healthy. Running wild in the marketplace or going to bed late will throw off their constitution."

"What's a *constitution*?" Naomi asked.

Delilah didn't answer and kept her attention on Leah. "And a child with questions is not busy enough."

Leah's face flushed even more than it already had.

Delilah lifted her rather narrow chin at Martha. "Where is your sister?"

No cheerful conversation tonight, it seemed. "Mary will be along soon," Martha said. "Now, if the men are ready, we can begin serving."

Delilah gave a brisk nod and picked up the platter with sliced barley bread and spicy goat cheese. Leah led the way, even though her step was slower. Martha shouldn't have been surprised to see Horeb, but there he sat, among the male guests. He'd become a part of the family in such a short amount of time. Isaac's two young sons sat among the guests as well, close to Rhode and Nathaniel, and seemed perfectly well-behaved.

Martha returned to the cooking room to share in the preparations for the next course. Mary really should be with them, specifically serving Isaac, her future husband. But Martha tried not to feel anxious because she didn't want Delilah to catch on. Mary was Mary, and she'd appear soon enough and be her sweet self.

But as the evening progressed and the men were nearly finished with the main course of fish and garden greens, Martha caught Leah's questioning gaze more than once.

"I'll be back," Martha mouthed to her sister-in-law and slipped out of the cooking room while Delilah was asking Leah how finely they'd ground the barley for the bread.

Martha hurried up the stairs to the second landing, her heart thudding with each footstep. Her heart had already climbed to her throat before she reached Mary's door. Fully expecting to confront a crying sister, Martha tapped on the door, then opened it.

The oil lamp burned in the corner, cutting the darkness with its soft glow. Martha didn't see her sister immediately, so she searched the bed. Had she cried herself to sleep as a child might? No, the bed linens held no such shape.

Dread pulsing in her stomach, Martha crossed to the window. What she saw made the blood rush to her head and her limbs tremble. A length of cloth had been tied to the hook near the window, and like a previous nightly sojourn, the cloth extended through the window and down the side of the house.

Mary was gone.

Breathe. Think.

Breathe. Think.

But Martha could do neither. Mary had fled on the night of her betrothal. The house was full of guests. Her husband-to-be was probably drinking wine with Lazarus in celebration of a long and healthy marriage.

Martha leaned over the windowsill and gazed down at the courtyard below. Where had Mary gone? Where had she fled to? And how would Martha tell everyone?

"Mary," Martha called into the night as loudly as she dared. "Come back, please. Let's talk about this. Mary?"

Was her sister close enough to hear? The only response to her pleas was the cool wind and deepening night. Moment after moment passed, and Martha knew she'd delayed long enough. She couldn't very well escape out the same window Mary had. Besides, Lazarus and Isaac deserved an explanation.

So Martha tucked in a few tendrils of her hair that had escaped her mantle and left the bedchamber. She went down the stairs, then walked through the cooking room without answering any of Delilah's or Leah's inquiries. She headed straight into the gathering room, and when Lazarus looked up, she motioned for him to follow her.

Immediately, her brother's brow furrowed since this was completely unexpected. But he excused himself and rose, then followed Martha to the private family quarters. In the dim corridor, she turned to face him. "She's left, Lazarus. Out the window. I called for her, but there's no answer. Do you want me to go and search?"

"I can search," another voice said.

Both Martha and Lazarus turned to see Horeb.

He raised both hands. "I'm sorry if this is a family matter, but I saw the distress on your face. With Mary not appearing, I wondered if something might be wrong . . . with her." He looked from one of them to the other. "No one will notice my absence, and perhaps I can help Mary see reason—"

"How do you know Mary needs to see reason?" Martha asked, not sure if she was annoyed or grateful at Horeb's intrusion.

"He was with me when Isaac spoke to me about Mary," Lazarus said.

Martha exhaled carefully and glanced at her brother. "Horeb doesn't know where to look, and he's not familiar with the village."

"Tell me where to look then," Horeb said.

The man was determined if nothing else. So Martha told him the places she thought her sister might go when distressed. She included the synagogue in her list, and Lazarus looked like he wanted to ask more questions.

"Very well," Horeb said. "I'll return soon with Mary."

Martha thought his promise was very confident, but Lazarus seemed to accept it. When Horeb disappeared down the hall, Lazarus sighed. "I'm afraid we have a long night ahead of us if Mary doesn't return very, very soon."

Martha pressed her lips together and nodded in agreement. It had already been a long night. She walked with Lazarus back through the house. He joined the men, and Martha entered the cooking room.

Leah's gaze met hers, but Martha didn't want to say anything in front of Delilah. At least not yet . . .

The next hour dragged on with Martha jumping at every sound that made her think someone had arrived at the house. Horeb did indeed arrive, but not with Mary. With so much time passing, it had become impossible to delay telling the truth any longer.

As expected, Isaac was furious. At least, his nearly scarlet face showed his anger, although he'd taken the news with calmness. When Isaac and the remaining guests left, Martha sank onto a cushion in the gathering room.

She didn't speak, didn't move as Lazarus and Leah worked to get the children settled down for the night. Horeb was pacing the courtyard outside. The only thing they hadn't tried was alerting the elders and forming an official search for Mary.

Martha felt deep inside that Mary was only hiding and hadn't actually left the village. Martha closed her eyes and drew her knees up. She mouthed the words to a prayer to Adonai, pleading that Mary would return and praying that all would be well in the end. Whatever that ending might be.

No longer did Martha think she and her brother should persuade Mary to enter into a marriage of which she was petrified. Her fears had been genuine—that Martha knew—but she hadn't expected them to be so strong.

Martha feared many things, yet she hadn't ever sneaked out of her home to escape those fears. She hadn't risked her reputation or the family's good name.

But right now, as the night crept on, Martha's fears changed from how Isaac might take action and publicly reject Mary to how the village might gossip and shun and finally to Mary's safety and well-being. Somewhere out there, her sister was alone and weeping.

Lazarus came into the room just as Martha rose to her feet.

"We need to go search again," she said, wiping at the tears on her face.

Her brother's expression had changed many times that evening. Right now it was resigned. "All right, but I think we might need more than just you, Horeb, and me."

"No," Martha said. "The more who are involved, the greater the expectation."

He paused at this. "You're right, but the hour is late, Martha. What if . . ." He looked away and closed his eyes for a moment. Then he said, "What if she's left Bethany? What if she is harmed by a wild beast or . . . ?" His voice fell. "Runs into bandits?"

Martha swallowed back her emotion. "I know someone who could help. Someone who wouldn't make everything worse."

Her brother's full attention was on her.

"Zachary," Martha said in a quiet voice. "He's the shepherd who uses David's land. Mary and I took herbs to his sick daughter earlier today."

Lazarus frowned. "How do you know this man?"

"I don't," Martha rushed to say. She explained about giving him suggestions in the market and then later learning his daughter had grown much worse.

Her brother nodded, although his jaw was clenched. "All right, then. We will seek out this Zachary."

Lazarus went to speak with Leah, and by the time he returned, Martha had donned a warmer robe and carried a rug for Mary. Who knew what state she'd be in and whether she'd left with warm clothing?

Horeb paused in his pacing as they exited the house. Once Lazarus told him of their plan, they headed with Martha in the direction of the fields on the other side of the village. Martha's heart ached, and her stomach felt hollow. She just wanted Mary to be safe. Nothing else mattered right now.

The walk to Zachary's tent felt like it took hours instead of minutes, and as they moved through the copse of trees, lit only by moonlight, Martha doubted her errand.

But a cooking fire on the other side of the tent, its smoke moving with the wind, gave her hope that at least all was well with Claudia.

Sure enough, they found Zachary crouched before the fire, stirring something in a pot. Next to him sat a small form bundled in a rug. But a third person was there as well.

"Mary," Martha cried out with a gasp. "You're . . . *here.*"

She rushed forward and pulled Mary to her feet, then tugged her into an embrace. Martha hadn't meant to cry, but her emotions spilled over all the same.

"I thought you'd never speak to me again," Mary murmured, her own voice trembling.

"What were you thinking?" Martha asked, drawing back to study her sister.

Zachary had risen to his feet, and no one else was speaking.

Mary took a shaky breath and stepped away from Martha, although she kept a hand latched on to her arm.

"Zachary was helping me," Mary said. "He told me I had to go back and honor my commitment. I agreed. But I needed some time to think. Lazarus, he said all the things you told me, and although I feel terrible about my actions tonight, I also feel better."

Lazarus rubbed a hand over his jaw, and Horeb just looked back and forth from Zachary to Mary as Zachary stared at the ground.

"What are we to tell Isaac?" Lazarus said at last.

"I cannot be his wife," Mary whispered.

"Because of Zachary?" Lazarus asked.

Zachary's chin snapped up. "There is nothing between us. Mary only came here—"

"Lazarus," Mary said. "This has nothing to do with another man. Not with Zachary or Isaac. Zachary was a stranger until yesterday, when Martha and I helped him with his daughter." She stepped forward, her eyes focused, her voice firm. "I know I have hurt the family. I have hurt Isaac's family too. But I'd rather be unmarried than marry him. I can remain in your household and help Leah in all things. I know that is unconventional, and I know I don't have the circumstances such as Martha . . . but, Lazarus, I know without a doubt that if I marry Isaac, I will fade away. My very heart will stop beating. Yet, I am sorry I have disappointed so many people."

No one responded as her words hung heavy and everyone waited for Lazarus's decision.

"You are safe, Mary," Lazarus said, his voice a rasp. "That is what's important. And you will always have a home with us."

CHAPTER ELEVEN
Mary

THE RAY OF LIGHT CRAWLED across the bedchamber as Mary watched. Yesterday it had been slightly to the left of the crack in the wall. Today the ray was nearly on top of the crack. And tomorrow, when Mary would be lying in her bed, unable to join the family in any meal or help Leah with any task, Mary would watch the ray pass over on the right of the crack.

Mary had barely left her bedchamber in weeks.

Everything inside of her felt empty. Gone. Even her thoughts were full of nothing.

She listened to the sounds of the house. Leah's voice speaking to her children. Naomi's higher-pitched one sometimes punctuated with a giggle. The sounds of the house changed when Rhode and Nathaniel were home. Martha had scolded them more than once about something, but her tone was affectionate.

Then Lazarus. His deeper voice rougher yet patient as always. Humble on the outside and inside.

Mary had thought she'd even heard Horeb a time or two. But she was pretty sure he still wasn't living in the house like Lazarus had offered.

She listened to the sounds coming through the window from the outside. The rush of the wind. The single day of rain. The winter swallows and their warbling, which she'd once found cheerful but which was, in fact, melancholy.

The rise and fall of the sun alternating with the moon was the only way Mary knew time had passed.

That and Martha appearing three times a day with food and drink.

Footsteps sounded now, and Mary recognized her sister's tread. She made no move to rise, to even turn, or to look away from the ray of sun that created a streak of orange on the wall across from her bed.

The door to her bedchamber clicked open.

The footsteps grew closer until Martha's tunic came into view.

Still, Mary didn't look up. Martha would move soon enough, and Mary would see the ray of light again. Was it the same ray each day from the same part of the sun? Or was it a different ray each day?

Martha set down a tray on the low table she'd brought in two weeks ago. Without looking at it, Mary already knew it was a slice of fresh barley bread and a platter of honey-soaked dates. The smells of each were distinctive.

But Martha did not move so that Mary could watch the ray. In fact, she sat on the edge of the platform bed and clasped her hands.

So . . . Martha was to try to start a conversation today, like she had various times during the first few days Mary had kept to her room.

Everyone in the household had visited her then. Everyone had offered comfort, sweet words, and Naomi had even sung a few songs. The songs had only made Mary cry, and Leah had led her daughter from the room.

Lazarus had spent hours at her bedside, holding her hand and carrying on a one-sided conversation. He hadn't seemed bothered that Mary had not replied. No, but Lazarus did tell her he'd spoken to Isaac. The betrothal would not take place. Isaac had told her brother he would not wait for Mary's ailment to pass.

It was just as well. Mary would probably never walk the streets of Bethany again without feeling judgment and censure in the villagers' gazes. Lazarus had said she'd always have a home with him, and that had allowed her to let go of the panic and fear. Yet letting go had also crippled her. It wasn't that she didn't want to climb out of her bed and leave the room. She wanted to be in the cooking room, helping Leah. She wanted to work side by side with Martha throughout the day. She even wanted to feed the goats. Walk the fields. Browse at the marketplace. Most of all, she wanted to sit outside the windows of the synagogue and listen to the teachings.

Yet her scrolls sat neglected in their corner, dust gathering.

"Mary," Martha said, her tone soft. "I have news."

News. What was news to her? A new babe born to a happy couple? A runaway goat? A caravan passing by that sold perfumes she'd never wear?

Mary closed her eyes. News didn't matter to her. Her sister would tell her, then her sister would leave, and then Mary would watch the ray finish moving across the room. She'd watch the walls turn violet and gold as the sun set, then she'd watch the walls shift to gray and finally indigo as the moon rose.

"Mary," Martha said again as she stroked the side of her face.

Her sister's touch was soothing, and Mary wasn't sure why she deserved such a wonderful family. Why couldn't she be like other young women and have the desire to be a wife and mother and be productive from sunup to sundown, falling to sleep each night with satisfaction and fulfillment?

Instead, the emptiness only grew.

Martha's hand moved to Mary's shoulder, and she rubbed a slow circle. "Lazarus has just returned from Jerusalem."

Mary knew this. He'd traveled there to trade at the larger markets this week.

"The city is abuzz with stories of Jesus and His miracles."

Mary opened her eyes at this. She did not move, did not speak, but a story about the man who'd healed Horeb was worth paying attention to. Martha surely saw the interest in her eyes because she continued.

"He has been in Samaria teaching that the law of Moses has been fulfilled. He has been performing miracles." Martha's hand continued to run slow circles over Mary's shoulder. "The people are saying He is headed this way."

Mary blinked.

"And Lazarus and Horeb are preparing to leave Bethany and possibly find him again." Martha paused. "Lazarus wants to invite Him to Bethany."

Something edged into Mary's mind. First the words of her sister, then the feeling they brought. A warmth. A lightness replacing the darkness that had dulled her thoughts. "When?" she whispered, her voice rough and cracked.

"Soon." Martha grasped her hand. "Lazarus says he will bring Him to the house to meet you."

Tears burned Mary's eyes. Her brother wasn't going to make her parade herself in front of the villagers . . . but would Jesus consent to come into one of the houses? A man such as He?

"I know what you're thinking, dear sister," Martha said, a soft smile on her face. "Even Jesus has to eat and rest. We will feed Him well, and then we'll hear His teaching and witness miracles for ourselves."

Mary nodded. She wanted to be a witness. She wanted to know that the broken could be made whole, and perhaps that might extend to her. There were so many questions she wanted to ask Him.

"Do you think He can help me?" Mary whispered.

"Of course," Martha said. "He can help us all."

Mary thought about this, and the warmth spread to more parts of her soul. "I should bathe," she said. "And organize my scrolls so that I know what to ask Him."

Martha's smile grew. "Both would be a very good thing. I will go with you to the bathing tent. No one will be there this time of morning."

"Is it still morning?" Mary asked.

"Yes, and we can take the back roads so we don't encounter anyone."

Mary squeezed her sister's hand. "Why are you so good to me? I should be sent to the streets and made to beg for my keep."

Martha shook her head. "Don't say that, sister. You might not remember, but when I moved back here after Yosef's death, you helped me more than you might know."

Mary pushed up on her elbow, gazing at her sister. "I did nothing. Leah was the one making your tea and helping you in the garden."

"Remember all the people who kept coming over, and you would speak to them, then send them away?"

Mary nodded. She did remember the women who stopped by to offer their condolences. But Martha had told her that she wanted to work through things quietly, staying busy with tasks and not beleaguering the situation with conversation about how wonderful her husband had been and how much he'd be missed.

Martha patted Mary's hand. "I had to stay busy and not dwell on Yosef every minute of the day. I didn't want an audience to watch me grieve."

"Well then, you're welcome," Mary said.

Martha laughed.

And surprisingly, Mary did too.

"Come," Martha said. "Let's hurry to the bathing tent. Perhaps Leah will want to come too."

As Mary rose from her bed and dressed, then joined Martha downstairs, she felt like she'd risen from a grave. Everything in the household looked the same yet different somehow.

"Leah must have gone to the market with Naomi," Martha said. "They're both gone. I wouldn't be surprised if she's getting things for Jesus's visit."

Oh, how Mary wished Jesus's visit would come to pass.

The air had warmed from the last time Mary had stepped foot outside. She'd missed the sun on her face, the breeze against her neck, and sights and sounds she hadn't been around. Thankfully, it was as Martha had said. The back roads were quiet, and as the sisters walked arm in arm, they only encountered Phebe, who simply nodded a greeting and hurried past.

"Is she afraid of me?" Mary whispered to Martha.

Martha laughed quietly. "She should be afraid of me more than you. I have been the one to stop gossips at our door this time."

Mary looked at Martha with surprise. She should have assumed this, but she hadn't thought it through. "Have there been many who've come to speak to me?"

"Not anyone as of late," Martha said. "But in the first week, you were definitely the interesting one in the village. Although, truly, the inquiries were ones of compassion. We didn't tell anyone that your betrothal would not be happening. Most assumed it would only be delayed. But now . . . I think Delilah has spoken her mind enough that the news is out"

Mary exhaled and tucked closer to her sister. "I am grateful to you and Leah. And our brother, Lazarus. He could have sent me away."

Martha only tightened her hold on Mary. "He would never do that. Not our brother."

The bathing tent was indeed empty, although it might not last long. Mary was grateful for the privacy from other women who might use her excursion as an item of gossip. They paid the young woman at the entrance, the keeper of the baths, then walked inside.

The air was warm and steamy despite the cooler temperature outside. Two low fires burned, keeping pots of water warm at all times. The inside of the tent had sections curtained off where the women would disrobe, then use the warm, sweet-scented water to cleanse their bodies. Once they had washed, they used clean swatches of cloth to dry off.

Mary applied oil to her hair, separating the strands, then running her fingers through. She used the jug of warm water to wash most of it away, leaving her hair silky and smooth. She felt renewed and clean as she left the bathing tent with her sister. Her step seemed lighter, and her heart had begun to fill with hope again. With the knowledge that Jesus of Nazareth might visit soon, Mary wanted to prepare right away. She needed to review her scrolls.

Mary's urgency increased as they walked back home, and it only compounded when she saw that Lazarus had returned. He met them at the door and quickly scanned Mary's face. "Leah didn't know where you'd gone . . . but you're all right?"

Mary nodded. "We went to the bathing house." The concern mixed with relief in her brother's eyes made her feel like crying again. But she wouldn't. "Martha told me that you went to find out more about Jesus's traveling plans."

Lazarus smiled. "Yes, and we have good news. Come in. Horeb is here as well."

Mary was definitely curious now as she followed her brother into the gathering room. It had been weeks since Mary had seen Horeb, and she wondered what he thought of her keeping to her bedchamber.

His smile was warmer and his countenance brighter than she remembered. She wondered if he'd always been this cheerful and positive or if it had happened after his healing.

Lazarus left to fetch the rest of the family, and Mary hesitated before sitting on a cushion because Horeb was approaching her.

"How are you, Mary?" he asked.

It was a simple question, but the warmth of his brown eyes seemed to sink into her heart and nestle there. She knew he wasn't asking how she was doing as a person at the market might, but he was asking because he was truly interested. His compassion was palpable.

"I am doing well," she said. "I have many blessings to be grateful for."

His smile was soft as their gazes remained locked. "My prayers have been answered, then."

Before Mary could let that sink in or come up with a reply, Rhode and Nathaniel came into the room. Both boys hugged Mary, and she kissed their cheeks. They said nothing about her sudden appearance in their lives again but argued over who could sit on an apparently favorite cushion.

Mary smiled, and Martha said, "That's enough."

Rhode won out, proclaiming he was the eldest, but it was only because Nathaniel relented as the peacemaker out of the two.

Mary found a cushion and settled on it to wait while Lazarus brought the rest of the family around. She was keenly aware of Horeb's thoughtful gaze on her even as he talked to Rhode and Nathaniel about working in the groves. Everything Horeb said led Mary to believe he was enjoying the work immensely. She was still curious about where he lived and slept, but she wouldn't ask that in front of everyone.

"Great, everyone's here," Lazarus said, walking in with Naomi on his hip and Leah following. He set Naomi down, and she scrambled onto Mary's lap.

"You're all better?" she asked, wrapping her tiny arms about Mary's neck.

Mary's throat was too thick to swallow properly, so she whispered, "I hope so."

Naomi smiled and only clung tighter. When Mary looked over at Leah, her sister-in-law was beaming at her.

Mary exhaled slowly. Her family members meant so much to her. They had accepted her plight and hadn't treated her harshly when she'd failed so deeply.

"First," Lazarus said, "I'm happy that Mary is among us today because I have something to report."

Mary didn't have time to blush at the attention because the next thing he said stunned everyone.

"Jesus will come to Bethany tomorrow," Lazarus said. "And He will be a guest in our home."

Mary gasped along with the others.

"Horeb and I just spent the morning with Him," Lazarus said. "He's staying the night not too far from Bethany, and then He'll travel here in the morning. Because of His remarkable gifts, a lot of people follow Him, and of course, His Apostles are with him all the time."

His expression turned somber. "Jesus also has naysayers—those who believe He is gaining too much notoriety. And they resent Him and His followers."

Mary frowned. "You have told us He is a man of miracles."

"He is," Lazarus confirmed. "Not everyone is happy with His miracles. They feel threatened by them. Joseph ben Caiaphas, the high priest, has claimed that Jesus has overstepped His bounds. Some followers have called Jesus the King of the Jews."

This made the family fall silent.

"Will there be a rebellion?" Rhode asked.

"Jesus brings peace to all," Lazarus said. "He will not head up a rebellion, and neither will His followers." He clasped his hands together. "Because of unseen danger, Jesus will only be in Bethany for a day. We should plan on feeding Him and His Apostles. The other followers will probably go to the market and make their own trades."

"We have so much to prepare," Leah said, her tone one of amazement.

Mary could practically feel the tense energy coming off Martha and Leah. Because of Leah's condition, surely she couldn't expect to do much of the work. It would be up to Mary and Martha.

"Before any plans are made," Lazarus continued, "we'd like to share the parable Jesus taught this morning. As you know, He has been spending time in Samaria."

Mary was more and more intrigued.

"Jesus teaches that all men and women are of the same fold," Lazarus said. "We are all brothers and sisters, and we shouldn't put one person above another." He nodded to Horeb. "Would you like to share the parable?"

Horeb looked surprised, but that didn't cause him to hesitate. "The crowds that surround Jesus are mostly His followers, but sometimes the doubters are there too—Pharisees and scribes and others who are looking for weaknesses and faults to complain about." He peered around the family circle. "Judgment of others surrounds us at every turn. Jesus is not exempt from the cruelest criticism and judgment. A lawyer among the crowd of people this morning stood and asked Jesus how he could inherit eternal life."

Mary stared. What was the answer?

"Jesus then asked the lawyer: 'What is written in the law? How readest thou?'"

Lazarus nodded his agreement as Horeb continued. "And Jesus said, 'Thou shalt love the Lord thy God with all thy heart, and with all thy soul, and with all thy strength, and with all thy mind; and thy neighbour as thyself.'"

Mary nodded as Horeb spoke, caught up in the words *with all thy strength* and *all thy mind.*

"But the lawyer had more questions," Lazarus added. "He asked Jesus, 'Who is my neighbour?'"

Horeb smiled at this. "And that's when Jesus shared the parable of a compassionate Samaritan."

Rhode leaned forward, his interest piqued. "What did Jesus say?"

Horeb glanced at Lazarus, who nodded for him to continue. "Jesus answered with a parable about a man who traveled from Jerusalem to Jericho but was beset by thieves."

"They're the bad men," Naomi said, her attention riveted as well as she turned her face away from Mary to watch Horeb.

"Yes," Horeb said. "These thieves were bad. They stripped him of his clothing and possessions, then they wounded him, leaving him half dead on the roadside."

Naomi looked up at Mary, her eyes rounded. Mary herself was intrigued. She knew it was only a parable, but what was Jesus trying to say?

"A priest came along," Horeb continued, "and when he saw the wounded man, he passed along the other side of the road so he wouldn't have to help him. Next came a Levite. The Levite saw the wounded man, but he didn't want to help either, so he continued down the road."

"Both men wouldn't help?" Naomi asked in her small voice.

"That's right," Horeb said. "Next, a certain Samaritan journeyed along the road and came across the wounded man. The Samaritan stopped and decided to help the man. So he bound up his wounds, using oil and wine, then he helped the man onto his donkey."

"Where did he take him?" Naomi asked, thoroughly entranced.

Horeb smiled. "The Samaritan took the wounded man to an inn, where he took care of him. And when the Samaritan had to leave the next day, he gave the innkeeper two pence and asked the innkeeper to care for the wounded man. The Samaritan also told the innkeeper that he'd pay him back for any expenses when he returned."

Mary thought of the priest and the Levite who hadn't wanted to bother with a wounded man. They'd rather leave him on the side of the road, near death, than stop and help. Yet the Samaritan, a man who was considered an enemy in their country, had been the one to stop.

"Jesus then looked at the crowd listening to Him and said, 'Which now of these three, thinkest thou, was neighbour unto him that fell among the thieves?'" Horeb paused. "Do you know what the lawyer answered?"

"The Samaritan," both Rhode and Nathaniel said at the same time.

"Right," Lazarus said. "The lawyer answered, 'He that shewed mercy on him.'"

"What did Jesus say after that?" Naomi piped up.

Lazarus's smile was filled with emotion. "'Go, and do thou likewise.'"

No one spoke for a few moments after that.

Mary thought of the times she'd helped others, her neighbors, her family members, someone in need she didn't know. The number and occasions were frightfully small. She could think of how Leah served everyone in the family and how Martha worked in their home as well as serving those outside their family circle. Lazarus too. And they'd served her personally as well. The entire family had served her for two weeks while she could barely open her eyes.

She felt Horeb's gaze on her, and when she looked over at him, instead of seeing censure, she only saw compassion. Her cheeks warmed, and she looked down at Naomi, who was still snuggled in her lap.

The family quietly discussed the parable of the compassionate Samaritan while Mary's thoughts tumbled. She wanted to do better. Be more aware of others. Return the love she'd been given.

CHAPTER TWELVE
Martha

MARTHA HADN'T SLEPT, OR AT least she didn't think so. It seemed she'd been aware of every hour that had passed during the night. She'd noticed the filtering moonlight as it shifted in the darkness of her bedchamber. Today was the day . . . although dawn had yet to soften the black sky, Martha knew it was close. She could feel it.

Was Jesus awake right now? Breaking camp? Traveling toward Bethany? How many would be traveling with Him? He had Apostles to think of as well. And that brought Martha's thoughts to the food preparations she'd been doing all the previous day after Lazarus and Horeb had told the parable of the compassionate Samaritan.

The story hadn't left her mind as she thought about how she'd shut out the caring people after Yosef's death. And how she still shut them out. True, she interacted with her siblings and Leah and her children, but Martha held herself apart more than she shared.

The Samaritan had helped a stranger without thought of the cost of both money and time. When was the last time Martha had done that? Zachary and Claudia leapt to her mind. She had done some good, something small. Would Claudia have recovered without Martha's interference? She would never know. But the gratitude in Zachary's eyes had been enough for Martha to know she'd done the right thing.

Is that what Jesus had meant? Serving someone, regardless of who they were, like you would your own family member?

When Martha arrived in the cooking room to get an early start on the chores in preparation for Jesus and His Apostles' arrival, she found Mary at the kitchen, cutting vegetables for a stew. The room was aglow from the fire in the hearth, but no one else was about.

"Couldn't sleep either?" Mary said in a soft voice.

Martha smiled. "Hardly." She was glad to see that the color had returned to Mary's cheeks and the brightness in them was coming back. Although suffering through the canceled betrothal hadn't been ideal, all in all, seeing her sister returning to health was the most important thing.

Mary continued her chopping, a soft smile on her face. "What do you think He'll look like?"

Martha raised her brows. She hadn't exactly thought about that. She assumed . . . what had she assumed? "I don't know. I'm not even sure how old He is."

Mary paused in her work and rested her chin on her hand as she gazed toward the fire. "He seems so full of love and kindness."

Martha nodded, even though her sister wasn't looking at her.

"It's a wonder that He travels like a vagabond," Mary said. "Lazarus told me He sleeps most nights outside and has no home of His own. His family home is in Nazareth, but He spends very little time there."

"By traveling, He can reach more people, I suppose." Martha's gaze was caught by the fire in the hearth as the flames sputtered and crackled. They had no idea what time Jesus would arrive, but they'd need to be ready to serve a meal to Him and those He traveled with. Martha turned to help Mary with the chopping, and once that was done, they worked on grinding more barley flour and making honey cakes.

By the time Leah was awake, the morning meal was already prepared. Rhode and Nathaniel stayed home from the synagogue to clean up the outer sections of the courtyard. Martha wished she could send Mary to the market for a few things, but she didn't know how Mary would fare out in public so soon.

Martha feared they'd run out of wine and other food supplies if they were to feed several men. When dawn had well passed and the morning proved to be cold and clear, Martha told the women in the cooking room that she wouldn't be long at the market.

Mary gave her a grateful look, and Leah nodded. "If there is winter fruit, buy some."

Winter fruit was expensive and a luxury they rarely indulged in. "Are you sure?"

"Yes," Leah said with a smile and handed over an extra pair of coins.

Martha thanked her and headed out the door. As she passed by Eunice's house, the woman paused in her sweeping of the mosaic tile surrounding the fountain in her courtyard.

"Have you heard the news?" Eunice asked. "Jesus of Nazareth is on His way. He's a man of many miracles."

Martha tried not to look stunned. She hadn't realized that word had spread to the neighbors, but when she reached the market, it was clear that everyone in Bethany knew about Jesus's miracles and expected His visit that day. Some women stood in groups, conversations hushed, while others haggled over food and wine with increased fervor. The men weren't in their fields or homesteads but milled about the market, anticipation in their expressions.

Martha bustled to the wine seller. He was rationing what he'd sell, so she purchased only two jugs of wine. Clutching them close, she crossed to Josiah's cart.

Josiah was perhaps the only merchant not encumbered with a crowd of people bargaining prices with him. Martha hurried over and met his wide-eyed gaze.

"Unless you have a family member ill," he said, "I don't have anything to offer today. It appears that the True Healer is about to take over my profession." His words weren't full of malice but of curiosity and skepticism.

"Josiah . . ." Martha said in a quiet tone so as not to be overheard. "Lazarus has invited Jesus to our home and—"

Josiah chuckled. "I'm sure everyone has invited Him to their homes. Good tidings to you."

Annoyed now, Martha walked around his cart to stand near him. Keeping her voice low, she said, "Josiah, I'm inviting you to our home to meet Him. I don't know when exactly He'll arrive, but when He does, we'll send word to you through one of Jesus's Apostles."

He frowned. "His Apostles?"

"Jesus has disciples he travels with," Martha said. "Lazarus and Horeb have met them. They act as protectors as well."

Josiah rubbed a hand over his chin, then focused on her. "That makes sense. Yes, send me word. I'd like to meet this Jesus of Nazareth."

Martha nodded, then turned to go.

"Wait," Josiah said.

When she looked back at him, he said, "Yesterday, Zachary visited my cart. He asked after you. He mentioned how you helped his daughter."

Martha hoped she was tamping down her rising blush so Josiah wouldn't see the curiosity burning inside her. She'd thought of Zachary and Claudia night and day, wondering how they'd fared. Still, she only visited the market in the mornings and not in the afternoons when she might encounter him.

"Claudia was with him," Josiah added.

Martha gave a small nod. "How does she fare?"

Josiah's smile was telling enough. "She's quite recovered, and it's no small matter. I believe you saved her life, woman."

She shook her head. "I was only following my instincts."

Josiah's gaze shifted past her, and his brows lifted.

Martha turned to see what he was gazing at. Zachary strode toward them, Claudia's hand clutched in his. Martha hadn't prepared herself for the moment when she'd see him next. Now, seeing him in the marketplace with Claudia at his side, looking sweet and healthy, stirred something in Martha's heart.

"You have heard, then?" Zachary asked with no preamble when he reached Josiah's cart.

Zachary's gaze was on her, although his words could have been for anyone.

"Yes, I have heard," Martha said, bending in front of his little girl. "And how are you?"

Claudia's smile was shy as she clung to her father's hand. "You're the one who helped me. Father told me you're an angel."

Martha's cheeks were surely heating, so she kept her gaze on the girl. "You are very blessed to have your health back. I'm glad to see you well."

Claudia scrunched her nose. "Is your sister still sad?"

Swallowing, Martha stalled, wondering how to answer the young girl when her father was listening. "She is having a good and busy day."

Yes, she felt Zachary's gaze on her, but she wasn't ready to look him in the eyes.

Claudia nodded enthusiastically. "Does that mean I can come and play with Naomi now?"

Martha had almost forgotten about that suggestion. "Well, yes, but not today, I don't think." She had no idea how long Jesus would be at their house. It was probably not the best time to have additional guests to worry over.

"We don't want to invite ourselves, Claudia," Zachary said in a quiet voice.

"But Mary said—" Claudia started to protest.

"It's all right," Martha quickly said, looking up at Zachary. "We would love to have her over anytime but . . ." She might as well confess since the whole of the village would know soon enough anyway. "Lazarus says that Jesus will be coming to our home today, and we are busy with preparations."

Speaking of preparations, Martha had already spent too much time at the market. She held Zachary's gaze, which was solely focused on her.

"I have heard of Jesus of Nazareth," Zachary said. "I've had a few conversations with Horeb about Him."

Martha couldn't look away from his dark eyes. "Yes, Horeb reveres Him above all else, and so does my brother."

"Horeb has made that clear." The edges of Zachary's mouth lifted into a slight smile. Thankfully, the intense worry on his face had fled, replaced with something like hope.

She smiled in return. "He has not been quiet about it in the least."

Zachary's eyes crinkled at the corners as his smile deepened. "No, he has not."

Martha felt a pull toward him. She wanted to step closer and share more conversation, but a hush fell over the marketplace as if everyone had been struck dumb at the same moment. Goose pimples skittered along Martha's arms before she'd turned fully to see what was going on.

"Father?" Claudia said in her tiny voice.

He hoisted her into his arms and stepped closer to Martha as they watched the crowds of the market part like a large hand had pushed them aside. Coming into the market square on the far side walked a group of men, the likes of whom Martha had never seen.

Their steps were slow but purposeful. Others crowded behind the smaller group of men, people who weren't from Bethany, but they were men and women alike.

Even though there were plenty of people to create a mob, the villagers merely watched in silence as the group entered the marketplace. Martha scanned each face until she stopped on one of the men, who'd paused in his step as a woman moved forward from the village crowd.

Martha recognized Tamara, the elderly woman whose hands wouldn't stop trembling. Recently, Martha had heard that Tamara's daughter-in-law had to administer food and water to her because Tamara couldn't even hold a cup.

The same man in the group paused and turned toward her.

Martha stared, her heart thumping. Somehow she *knew* that the man who'd paused was the man named Jesus. His robes were simple, a dark brown of loose weave. From this distance, she couldn't see His eye color, but His hair was deep brown and wavy against His shoulders.

"It's Jesus of Nazareth," Martha whispered to herself.

Zachary and Josiah said nothing, and Claudia kept her arms clutched around her father's neck.

Martha watched as Tamara held her hands out to Jesus. He clasped her hands in His. Martha was too far away to hear any words spoken, but she saw Tamara sink to her knees and bow before the man as her shoulders shook. Was she crying?

Even though Martha wasn't sure what had happened, her eyes burned with tears as her throat stiffened with emotion. The whispers started in the crowd, moving through the people until Martha heard them for herself: *Jesus has healed Tamara.*

Martha's breath left her chest. She wanted to rush to Tamara and see for herself, but she couldn't move her feet. Rooted to the ground, she watched a young man, Benjamin, hobble forward, gripping his cane, and beseech Jesus. Benjamin's leg had been broken the year before in a fall, and he'd used a cane ever since.

Again, Jesus spoke to the man, and when Benjamin sank to his knees without the use of his cane, Martha could only stare.

She looked over at Josiah to see if he was seeing the same thing. His eyes were focused on the scene, and his mouth was agape. Next, Martha looked at Zachary. He met her gaze, his eyes full of wonder.

The crowd seemed to part when another man who was rarely seen in public approached Jesus. Simon the leper had lost his living when he'd contracted the disease. His bandages might have been hiding his sores, but he was still fearsome to behold. Martha had often left food baskets at the door of his house, a small way to help provide for a destitute man.

With her heart climbing her throat, Martha watched as Simon the leper approached Jesus and beseeched him. The townspeople near Jesus stepped back, not wanting to be near an unclean man. Mothers ushered their children away, and a couple of men looked like they were about to force Simon to leave. But Jesus raised his hand as if to tell everyone to be at peace. Then He leaned toward Simon and spoke. Although Martha couldn't hear the conversation, soon Simon straightened, then tugged off his bindings.

It was as if the man had never contracted the disease. The people in the market murmured their astonishment as Simon laughed and cried about his healing. He held out his hands, examining the clear skin upon his fingers and palms. Then he touched his face and neck, finding them sore-free. "I am clean," he cried out. "I am clean."

His smile was brilliant as he gazed at the surrounding crowd. "Where is the priest? I must certify my cleanliness."

Tears ran freely down Martha's cheeks at the sight of the miraculous healing. Jesus was here. And He was performing miracles, ones she'd only heard about, before her very eyes.

Soon, Jesus would come to her home, another remarkable event. And she had nothing ready. At least not as much as she needed. He was healing people in the streets of Bethany while she stood by. She needed to provide Him a meal, and right now, Leah and Mary had no idea He'd arrived.

"I must go," Martha said in a rush to Zachary. "Jesus will expect a meal, and I've much to do."

"Do you need help carrying those wine jugs back to your home?" Zachary asked.

Martha didn't even have time to consider his offer. "I can carry them," she said, knowing she was possibly being discourteous by turning down his offer. Her thoughts were disjointed and wouldn't fully connect.

She took a step back, then another. Zachary merely watched her but said nothing. Then she turned and hurried from the market, clutching the wine jugs. She passed villager after villager heading in the opposite direction. Some of them asked if Jesus had truly arrived, but she only nodded, no longer having a voice to speak.

Questions circled in her mind. How long would Jesus be in the marketplace? When would He arrive at her home? Would all of His Apostles come inside and want to be fed? Should they set up an eating area in the back courtyard? Yes, that would probably be best. But the air was chilly, and surely the men would be more comfortable inside.

She didn't know where Lazarus or Horeb were either. Maybe they had heard fresh news? What had Jesus said to them exactly? By the time she entered the cooking room from the back of the house, she was perspiring, and her pulse was thudding. Both Mary and Leah were in the cooking room, and they looked over at her in expectation.

"He's here," Martha said, not explaining who "He" was. "I saw Him in the marketplace. He healed Tamara, Benjamin, and Simon the leper before my very eyes. Nothing is ready, and He could arrive at any moment. What will we feed Him?" All of the anticipation and emotions caught up with her, and she burst into tears.

Mary hurried over and took the wine jugs from her arms before she dropped them.

Martha sank onto a bench and buried her face in her hands. Leah moved close and rubbed her back. "We have all the food, Martha. We only need to begin preparations now. You've brought enough wine, and we can feed Jesus and His Apostles olives, figs, cheese, and bread while we work on the rest of the meal."

Martha was still crying, but she nodded. "All right," she said over a choked voice. "Let's begin the platters so that we have something ready the moment they arrive." She lifted her head and wiped at her cheeks. "What about the washing basins? They need to be prepared. Surely they'll want to wash after their journey."

"Yes," Leah soothed. "Mary, can you fetch all of the basins in the house? Heat water over the fire, and when you fill the basins, add our best oils."

Martha took several deep breaths as Leah gave out instructions. There were three of them; they could do this. It wasn't all up to her. The moments sped by nearly as fast as her heart rate.

Mary prepared the basins while Leah mixed the honey cakes and set them to bake. Martha arranged the platters, then speared fish on skewers and set them over the fire in the hearth. They'd need tending and turning every so often. Martha hurried to the gathering room and peered out the front door. No sign of anyone arriving yet. She called for Rhode and Nathaniel, but they didn't answer. Perhaps they'd followed the crowds to the market.

Reentering the gathering room, Martha set about arranging cushions. Then she lit oil lamps although the sun was still up. Next she burned incense, letting the aroma waft through the room and give everything a sweet, calm scent.

The next moments turned into an hour, then two hours, and still Martha felt like they were behind in all the preparations. When the front door opened, Martha paused while stirring the stew. She released the long spoon and stepped away from the hearth. Voices. She heard men's voices.

Mary caught her eye from across the cooking room, and Leah had raised her head from where she sat.

All three women paused, gazing at each other as the male voices threaded through the house and into the cooking room.

Lazarus spoke above the rest.

"Welcome to our home, Jesus," Lazarus said. "I will fetch water for you and your disciples."

Chapter Thirteen

Mary

Mary watched her sister's face flush, and she was sure her own cheeks had pinked. The murmur of male voices was not distinguishable, but it was clear their guests had arrived.

"Go," Martha whispered. "Go and see what's happening."

Mary's heart thumped at the request, but she was curious too, and her greatest wish was to converse with Jesus. Or, at the very least, hear His words in person.

"Father's home," Naomi said, climbing off the bench and running toward the gathering room.

"Naomi," Leah said in reprimand. "Do not—"

But Naomi had already disappeared from sight. Leah rose to her feet, but her expression told Mary she was reluctant to follow her daughter.

"We will go together," Mary said, linking her arm with Leah's, then nodding to Martha.

Her sister visibly swallowed, looking like she'd rather stay in the cooking room. "Come, Martha," Mary encouraged.

So the three of them entered the gathering room. Naomi had already made her way to her father and had wrapped her little arms about his legs where he stood just inside the doorway. "Leah," he said as soon as he saw her. "Come, all of you."

Mary walked forward with the women until they joined Lazarus in the doorway and could see the front courtyard, where several men had gathered. Beyond the walls of their courtyard, villagers lingered, watching and waiting, perhaps for their turn to greet these guests.

Mary scanned the faces of the men. There were about a dozen. At first, it wasn't immediately clear which was Jesus, but the moment she saw Him, she knew it was Him. hope

She couldn't explain it exactly, but the expression on His face and the warmth of His gold-brown eyes made it hard for her to look anywhere else. She was riveted by the sense of compassion and deep, abiding love she felt emanating from Him. She'd never laid eyes on this man, Jesus of Nazareth, but she felt He knew her with only one glance and no words.

Lazarus made introductions, but Mary barely heard what her brother was saying as he introduced the women of his family to Jesus and His Apostles. The names of Andrew, Peter, John, James, Matthew, Philip, and more swirled about her. Horeb had also arrived with the men, but he remained in the back of the group, keeping watch on the villagers beyond the wall as if guarding the house.

Jesus's benevolent gaze went to each person as Lazarus named his family members. Somehow Nathaniel and Rhode appeared, even though Mary hadn't seen them enter. As Lazarus made the introductions, Jesus repeated the names of each family member as if committing them to memory. And Mary guessed this was a man who didn't forget names.

"And this is Mary," Lazarus said. "My youngest sister."

The eyes of their guests shifted to her, and Jesus's gaze once again returned to hers.

Mary clasped her hands before her, wanting to kneel before Him but not knowing what was expected. Jesus repeated her name, and her eyes pricked with tears as unidentifiable emotions swept through her. He knew her name. That knowledge alone brought a joy to her heart, a joy she couldn't remember feeling before.

"We have fetched water for our guests to wash their feet," Leah murmured.

"Wonderful," Lazarus said. "We will return shortly with the basin of water."

Lazarus went with the women into the cooking room and helped carry the basins of water scented with oil. The men washed their feet in the scented water, then Lazarus invited them inside.

But the Apostle named Andrew said, "We will remain out here while Jesus rests inside."

And so it was. Mary watched Jesus walk into her home.

Lazarus led Him to a cushion at the end of the low table, where Jesus then sat. Mary watched Him settle, thinking of how this man had walked days and days to teach and heal people in need. His feet had carried Him that distance. And now He was resting in their home.

The conversations among the Apostles coming in from the window was low and mellow, and it seemed they were content to wait where they were.

"We are preparing a nice meal for you and your disciples," Martha said to Jesus.

Mary didn't miss the nervous tremor in her voice as she spoke.

But Jesus didn't seem to be in any hurry to eat. He thanked her, and Martha returned to the cooking room. Mary lingered in the gathering room to listen as Lazarus asked Jesus how He'd fared on the journey to Bethany.

Perhaps she wasn't welcome to listen in, but Jesus and her brother didn't seem bothered in the least.

"I shared the parable of the Samaritan with my family," Lazarus said, glancing at Mary.

She nodded, and Jesus's compassionate gaze turned upon her.

"I loved the story," Mary said, hoping she wasn't speaking out of turn. But Jesus only watched her with interest. "It made me realize that I should be looking for more opportunities to serve and not just those in my family. I have been caught up in my own woes lately and perhaps have neglected times when I could have assisted another."

Jesus nodded.

"But Horeb and Lazarus have both told me of your teachings," Mary said. "I have a great deal of trouble looking for the good in all things." She waited for His answer, holding her breath in anticipation. Would He find her comments foolish? But His next words told her He did not.

"Mary." Jesus spoke her name, then said, "Peace I leave with you, my peace I give unto you: not as the world giveth, give I unto you. Let not your heart be troubled, neither let it be afraid."

Mary was already crying. The words were comforting, and hearing Jesus tell her not to be troubled or afraid was somehow precisely what she needed in that moment.

She continued to ask Him questions, and Jesus gently answered each one, telling her some parables that she'd heard in different forms from her brother already. At one point, Lazarus went outside, and Mary assumed he was speaking with the Apostles.

She asked Him how she could stay stronger and not falter. Jesus didn't seem bothered by her weaknesses. He told her she didn't need to accomplish large feats but that the smaller things were just as welcome.

"If ye have faith as a grain of mustard seed, ye shall say unto this mountain, Remove hence to yonder place; and it shall remove; and nothing shall be impossible to you."

Mary wished she could write down every word Jesus spoke. She never wanted to forget His analogy of the mustard seed, for that was exactly how she felt in this world, yet Jesus had said that nothing would be impossible to her.

Martha came into the gathering room and set a tray with a cup of wine and plate of figs before Jesus. He thanked her, then drank and ate a little. Martha looked directly at Mary and motioned for her to follow her to the cooking room to help. But Mary couldn't very well leave when He'd been sharing so much wisdom with her. Mary shook her head so that only Martha would get the message.

Martha pursed her lips and returned to the cooking room alone. When Jesus began telling her a parable about a lost sheep, Mary was glad she hadn't followed her sister. "If a man have an hundred sheep, and one of them be gone astray, doth he not leave the ninety and nine, and goeth into the mountains, and seeketh that which is gone astray?"

Although Jesus was speaking of sheep, Mary knew He referred to everyone. She thought of how her family had taken care of her in her deepest sorrow; how Martha had taken care of Claudia without any payment or accolades; how Lazarus had helped Horeb in so many ways. Mary's gaze was solely fixed on Jesus as He continued.

"And if it so be that he find it, verily I say unto you, he rejoiceth more of that sheep, than of the ninety and nine which went not astray."

It was absolutely true; Mary had felt it in her own life.

Martha appeared again to refill Jesus's wine cup, although He hadn't finished all of it. She set down a platter of olives before Him. He took one and thanked her again.

Martha nodded, but her questioning gaze flitted to Mary, making it clear that she thought Mary should be helping in the cooking room. And Mary should, but when else would she have Jesus in her home and the chance to learn from Him?

When Mary shook her head again, Martha whispered, "Won't you help with preparations, sister?"

Lazarus hadn't returned from the courtyard, and surely the meal preparations could wait a short time.

"I will soon," Mary said, although she didn't want to move if Jesus was going to continue teaching.

Martha disappeared again. The scent of cooked meat was stronger, and Mary guessed the meal was nearly ready to be served. Mary would help serve.

Before she could excuse herself from Jesus, Martha entered the gathering room a third time, but she wasn't carrying the wine jug.

Martha stopped in front of Him and bowed. "Lord, do you not care that my sister has left me to serve alone? Perhaps she can help me now."

Mary went both hot and cold at the same time. Surely she would be reprimanded now. It was always the same. Her curiosity and interest in learning all she could always got her into trouble.

Jesus's smile was soft as He gazed at her sister. "Martha, Martha," he said in a quiet tone, "thou art careful and troubled about many things: But one thing is needful: and Mary hath chosen that good part, which shall not be taken away from her."

Martha said nothing for a moment, as if she were too stunned to speak.

Mary couldn't remember a time when anyone had suggested that learning of spiritual principles was more important than physical chores. But here the Lord had implied that Mary's persistence in learning was *needful*. Warmth seeped through her, and she looked up to see Lazarus standing in the doorway, his expression thoughtful.

Martha clasped her hands in front of her, then bowed her head. In the next moment, she returned to the cooking room. Mary felt breathless. Her choice had been validated.

Jesus hadn't criticized her sister but had explained that it was all right that Mary was spending time to learn things beyond her daily duties.

Mary nodded, feeling like her mind had expanded tenfold in just the short time she'd been listening to Jesus. Lazarus had left again, and Martha and Leah remained in the cooking room. Mary suspected that these few moments alone with Jesus were perhaps all she'd ever have, and she cherished each one.

She smiled, but her eyes also burned with tears.

Lazarus soon returned to the room and settled on a nearby cushion. Jesus nodded to her brother, then said, "If ye continue in my word, then are ye my disciples indeed; And ye shall know the truth, and the truth shall make you free."

Martha and Leah both appeared, carrying trays of soup in clay bowls, cooked fish, and steaming lentils. They set the meal before Jesus, then returned without a word to the cooking room.

Jesus began to eat, then invited Lazarus and Mary to join him. But Mary couldn't eat a thing. Not now. He and Lazarus spoke of Jesus's recent journeys, and Mary continued to listen with rapt attention.

Moments later, Martha and Leah carried food to the Apostles in the courtyard. As the women came back inside, Martha paused before returning to the cooking room. "Thank you for teaching my sister," she said, her voice cracking with emotion.

Mary was overjoyed when Jesus invited Martha to join them. With the slightest hesitation, Martha sat on the cushion next to Mary.

Mary grasped her sister's hand and squeezed.

Martha asked a few questions, and Jesus answered in His humble way.

Mary had never been so moved in her entire life as she watched Martha soak in the words of the Lord. The voice of Jesus was warm and calm, and His very tones brought peace to her heart. She could listen to Him all day, all night, and all the next day. As the midday shifted into afternoon, it was clear that Mary and Martha couldn't keep the man all to themselves.

Lazarus had left, and now entered with the Apostle named Andrew.

"A crowd has gathered," Andrew said.

Mary fully expected Jesus to say He hadn't rested yet because she had commandeered all of His time. Instead, He told Andrew that He would come straightaway. After bidding farewell to Mary and Martha, Jesus left the house and walked into the courtyard.

From inside the house, it was clear by the voices coming in that the crowd had grown significantly. So many of Jesus's followers were seeking His attention. And yet He'd spent an afternoon with just Mary and her family. For several moments, the sisters listened to the bustle of the crowd outside, neither of them speaking. Then Mary realized Martha was crying.

"What is it?" Mary asked, grasping her sister's hand.

Martha gave a tremulous smile. "I'm so very glad you chose the good part, Mary. As Jesus said, I encumber myself too much with chores. Sometimes I don't stop to listen when I should. And today, we are blessed beyond measure to hear the words of the Lord. Nothing can replace that in importance."

Mary swallowed against the emotion tugging at her throat. "Thank you, dear sister."

Martha pulled Mary close, and the two embraced.

They spent the next while making sure the Apostles were all fed in the courtyard. Jesus had already moved to the wall and greeted many of the villagers. Even the children were in awe of the man, and Jesus treated each child as if they were of great importance.

The scene was so tender it brought tears to Mary's eyes.

The afternoon wore on, and as the sun began its descent along the western sky, Jesus bade farewell to the family of Lazarus. He moved on from their house to travel to another location, and Mary watched from the courtyard, arm in arm with her sister.

The village was abuzz with all the miracles of Jesus. And although Mary hadn't had a limb perfected or an illness healed, she felt more whole than she'd ever felt before. She felt strong, joyful, and her previous woes felt lighter than they had in a long time.

"I am going back inside to rest and ponder all that we've been taught," Martha said.

Mary looked at her sister in surprise. "You're going to *rest*?"

"Remarkable, isn't it?" Martha smiled.

Mary laughed. "Yes, very."

Martha squeezed her hand, then left Mary in the courtyard. Clouds had gathered, and the wind had picked up with the progressing afternoon. Mary didn't mind. She wasn't cold at all, perhaps due to the warm words floating through her. They were words she held precious and would rely on when she was faced with challenges in the future.

She almost didn't notice Horeb coming along the road in front of the house until he stopped directly in front of her. Mary looked up to see him smiling at her.

"Did you see Jesus with the children?"

"Yes," Mary said. "He is truly a man of compassion."

Horeb's smile broadened. "We have a new way to live now, Mary. Our lives have a renewed purpose, and Jesus has promised us eternal life. That means I'll see my mother again."

The tender fact made Mary smile through threatening tears. "Yes, and I'll see my parents again."

Horeb opened the gate and walked into the courtyard. "I can never thank your family enough for what you have done for me. If it wasn't for Lazarus, I'd still be a poor man hobbling around Galilee, begging for a job."

Mary shook her head with amusement. By all appearances, Horeb still wore his threadbare clothing and looked as if he slept in the road at nights. "We are all blessed."

His gaze seemed to intensify, and Mary felt a sudden heat in her chest.

"You are right," Horeb said. "Now, if I can beg a favor from you, tell me what you and Jesus spoke about."

Mary arched a brow. "Do you not know all of His teachings? You are never quiet about them."

Horeb chuckled. "You have noticed. I thirst for knowledge, just like a young woman I know."

Her cheeks were likely flushed, but she didn't look away from him. "I do know that."

Horeb leaned against the wall and folded his arms as if he were patiently waiting for her to talk. Mary sighed, then perched on the wall a pace or two away from him. "I don't think any of it will be new to you, but perhaps you'll be able to give me additional insights."

"I'll try." He inclined his head. "But I am sure you have plenty yourself."

Mary wouldn't blush again; she refused to allow it. How could one man be so different from another? She could never imagine this conversation with Isaac. "Jesus taught me the mustard seed parable."

Horeb's expression brightened, but he didn't interrupt. It was clear he was already familiar with it. But as Mary spoke, he only listened and nodded. She'd been enjoying talking to him for so long that she didn't notice the darkening clouds until the rain started.

"You should come inside," Mary said. "The storm looks vicious."

"I'll be fine." Horeb straightened and moved through the gate again. "Thank you for sharing your experiences with me, Mary."

She nodded because she was speechless as she watched Horeb hurry away, pulling his threadbare robe closed against the wind. Mary doubted he'd stay warm tonight.

"Horeb, do you want me to weave you a new robe?" she called after him.

He turned, his brows raised. "That offer is too generous."

"I agree, but it's still a nice offer."

"All right," Horeb said with a grin. "I won't turn that down."

Chapter Fourteen
Lazarus

"You have done too much this week, Lazarus," Leah said as she brought him tea where he reclined on their platform bed. The few weeks after Jesus's departure had been busy with work in the olive groves. Spring was well on its way.

Horeb had been a hard worker, though, cheerfully putting in long hours. In fact, the entire village was in good spirits. Discussions at the synagogue were lively and full of deep introspection as the men and boys studied the psalms, laws, and prophets with renewed vigor and understanding. The skeptics also had a voice, making sure they were heard.

Now Lazarus was feeling the effects of an illness that had settled deep in his chest, but he was sure it would soon pass. "Thank you, Leah," he said, taking the tea and sipping at the hot brew. His cough had worsened over the past couple of days, but at home, he'd tried to keep his coughing as light as possible so as not to worry his wife.

Still, Martha had gone to the herbalist, Josiah, and requested various leaves and stalks. He'd had quite a variety of teas, but nothing seemed to be truly helping. A tickle worked its way down his throat, and he took another sip of the tea.

"I should be waiting on *you*, not the other way around," Lazarus said, eyeing his wife.

Her delivery was less than a month away, and he'd been praying night and day that she'd deliver safely and her health would remain intact.

Leah only smiled at him, her dark eyes as beautiful as ever. Then her smile faltered. Lazarus set his cup down and pushed himself up in the bed, although the movement caused him to wheeze. "What is it? Are you all right?"

She looked away with a short exhale. "I haven't felt well today. It's not like the illness you have, yet I can't explain it."

He reached for her hand and squeezed. "Is it the child?"

Her hesitation was long enough that Lazarus pushed off his covers and rose from the bed. His chest felt like it was on fire, but he didn't care.

"Lazarus, I'll be fine for a while yet," Leah protested, but her tone was weak.

"Where is Martha?" Lazarus moved about the room to fetch his robe. He tugged it on and ignored the steady burning in his chest. He covered his mouth with his sleeve and coughed deeply against the fabric.

"I can fetch her," Leah said, watching him with widened eyes. "You shouldn't be up—"

But Lazarus pointed to her. "You take the bed. I'll find Martha, and until I know *you* are well, I'll rest in the boys' room to be near you. They can move upstairs."

Without waiting for a reply, he left the bedchamber and called for Martha.

She must have heard the urgency in his tone because she hurried out of the cooking room, her hands dusted with flour. "What's happened?"

"Leah is having birthing pains." Lazarus's tone was perhaps too sharp. "Did you not know this? She said she's been ill all day."

"She's said nothing," Martha said. "I will check on her, but what about you?"

Lazarus threw up his hands. "I will be fine. My illness will pass. Please, right now my wife needs tending."

Martha hurried past him, and Lazarus went into the cooking room. He didn't know what he was looking for, but he couldn't lie in the bedchamber while Leah was about to deliver a child.

"Mary?" he called up the stairs, pushing his voice so he could be heard, which sent him into a coughing fit.

Her footsteps sounded soon after, and she appeared at the top. He told her about Leah, and Mary said, "I'll go fetch the midwife. Should I tell the boys at the synagogue?"

"No," Lazarus said. "They will be home soon enough." He paused for another fit of coughing. When he had control again, he looked at Mary's worried face. "Don't say it. I'll be fine. Just get the midwife."

Mary nodded and hurried down the stairs, then out the door.

Lazarus moved to the table and braced himself against it for a moment. His breathing was labored, which was irony in itself.

Time to check on Leah and see if there was anything he could do for her. He returned to their bedchamber, feeling weaker by the moment. When he reached the doorway, he leaned against the doorframe. Martha had helped Leah into bed.

Leah was perspiring, and her face was pale. How had Lazarus not noticed that before?

"You don't look so well," Martha told him. "You should lie down."

"I'm not lying down," Lazarus said. "I sent Mary to fetch the midwife, and I need to know what I can do to help you prepare."

Martha left Leah's side and moved closer to Lazarus. "You can rest and get better so you are healthy enough to meet your new child when he or she is born."

At that moment, Leah groaned.

Lazarus moved past his sister to his wife's bedside. "Are you in pain already?" He snapped his head to Martha. "Is she going to deliver soon?"

Martha set her hand on his arm. "Brother, she needs support, not panic. You look like you're about to collapse. Will you go lie down before I'm forced to nurse both of you and an infant?"

"Please," Leah said in a strained whisper. "Do as your sister says. I'm in good hands."

Lazarus still hesitated. Finally, he headed to the doorway. "I'll be in Rhode and Nathaniel's room. Let me know if you need anything."

"We will," Martha said. "And thank you for having Mary fetch the midwife."

Female voices sounded from the gathering room as Lazarus walked into the corridor. The midwife was already here. That was comforting news. He headed that way and nearly ran into Mary walking with an older woman.

"Tamara?" he said, surprised to see her here. She'd been a midwife years ago, but even with her miraculous healing by Jesus, Lazarus hadn't expected her to come help in his household.

"Rachel is with another in our village who is close to her time," Tamara said. "And Jesus's healing has left me more capable than ever." She tilted her head and studied him.

"You don't look so well. Mary said you've been ill."

"I want to help—" He cut off when a cry sounded from the bedchamber. Leah again.

Lazarus felt ill—ill at the thought of his wife's pain and ill because his limbs were so weak.

"We will take good care of Leah," Tamara said. "Leave the women's work to the women."

Mary and Tamara moved past him, leaving him once again alone in the corridor. The murmur of soothing women's voices now came from his bedchamber. Lazarus closed his eyes. He could do this. He could rest and regain his strength so that by the time his child was born, he'd be strong enough to hold him.

Or her.

Lazarus didn't care about the gender of the child, just that both mother and child were healthy. God had already blessed him with two strong sons and a beautiful daughter. Would the blessings continue? At Leah's next cry, Lazarus lumbered to his sons' bedchamber and practically collapsed onto one of the platform beds. He truly was exhausted, and although lying down helped, every part of his body ached. Even breathing was painful.

He closed his eyes, trying to breathe calmly—inhale, exhale. He needed strength and stamina. "Oh, God," he prayed. "Thank thee for all the blessings thou hast bestowed upon our family. Thank thee for sending thy Son to teach us the new way. Watch over my wife in her hour of need." Lazarus continued to pray, to plead, until he finally fell asleep.

"Lazarus," a voice said.

He wasn't sure if he was dreaming or awake, but someone was gently shaking his shoulder.

"Mary?" he whispered.

"It's Martha," his sister said.

Yes, he did recognize her voice, but he was so very tired. "What . . . time is it?"

"It's late at night," Martha said, her voice sounding somewhere above him.

He tried to open his eyes, but his eyelids were too heavy.

"Leah's delivered a healthy son," Martha continued, her hand on his shoulder again.

Lazarus opened his eyes this time and grasped his sister's hand. "I have another son," he breathed, triumph coursing through him. If only he could celebrate with his wife and share the good news with the neighbors. But his energy faded as quickly as it had gathered.

"You must rest, brother," Martha said.

"I know," Lazarus whispered.

The room was dim, likely lit with a single oil lamp somewhere. He didn't know where his other children were, but the house seemed quiet. Martha's dark eyes studied him.

"I've brought you some tea," she said.

Lazarus nodded but then winced as he tried to sit up. His neck ached, and that reminded him of how much his head hurt too.

Martha grasped his arm. "You need the healer."

"You know more than he," Lazarus grunted. He took a sip of the tea and swallowed, grateful it didn't make him cough. "He'll only light incense and chant. We know that the only one with the true power to heal is Jesus." Martha nodded. "We will keep praying, then."

Lazarus took another sip of tea. He felt a little better. Perhaps he was turning the corner. "Can I see my child now?"

"Of course." Martha took the cup and set it to the side, then extended her hand to help Lazarus to his feet. It should have been a simple thing, but it took an immense amount of effort.

But Lazarus didn't want his sister to worry more than she already had. He was a strong man, and he could walk to the next room. Still, Martha must have seen what he wasn't ready to admit, and she slipped her arm about his waist, offering support.

"I'm not an invalid, sister," he complained.

"Maybe not, but you're irritable when you're ill, dear brother."

The affection in her tone made Lazarus feel emotional again. How had he been blessed with such a patient family?

As they shuffled into the bedchamber, Lazarus was struck with the sweet peace that comes after the delivery of a new child. This babe might be his fourth child, but he was just as grateful as he had been with the first one.

Leah looked up from where she held the newborn against her breast. Leah's dark hair tangled about her shoulders, and although night had fallen and only a couple of oil lamps lit the room, her face glowed as if the midday sun was spilling in through the window.

"My dearest love," Lazarus murmured, his voice choking as tears rushed to his eyes. He swallowed against the threatening tickle in his throat and ignored the burning in his chest. Sitting next to Leah, he reached out a hand to rest on the crown of the babe's head.

"It's a boy," Leah said, her eyes on him, gauging his reaction.

"A boy, beautiful like his mother." He bent close and kissed the top of the babe's head, then kissed Leah's cheek. "You are well?"

Her shining eyes met his. "I am well. We will have to fight over who gets to rest more."

"I am recovering," Lazarus said.

Leah didn't look convinced.

"Martha is clever with her tea concoctions, and it's only a matter of time before I'm out in the groves again."

Leah nodded but was clearly still worried.

If anything, Lazarus would recover faster because he had so much to do, especially with a new child in the house.

"Have the others met their sibling?" Lazarus asked.

"Not yet," Leah said. "I wanted you to be the first."

Lazarus smiled at that. But then his chest seized, and he had to move off the bed as his body hacked. Amidst his chest spasms, he felt a hand on his back—Martha's. Then her voice murmured in his ear.

"Come, brother, let's get you back to resting."

It wasn't his first choice, but he didn't want Leah worrying about him. She had her own recovery to make. His vision blurred with tears of gratitude mixed with the pain of his burning chest and frustration with his weakened body. He was barely aware of Martha coaxing him to drink more tea, then telling him to lie down. He felt the flutter of her hands as she covered him with a warm rug. He wasn't cold, not in the least, but somehow he was comforted.

"Sleep, Lazarus," Martha said. "Do not concern yourself with anything but regaining your health. Your family will be here when you awaken."

CHAPTER FIFTEEN
Martha

MARTHA WALKED THE FLOOR WITH her fussy nephew held against her shoulder, only a patch of moonlight coming through the window of the gathering room to give her a view of where she was going. The infant had taken to waking in the middle of the night and not settling down after being fed by his mother. The child's cries had echoed through the house that night, and Martha knew she wouldn't be able to sleep anyway, so she had drawn on her robe and gone downstairs to help.

→ *Cayla* ←

She was sure Leah wasn't sleeping yet, but perhaps by the time the babe slept, Leah would finally be resting. Thankfully, Leah was healing and regaining her strength. Mary had taken over care of Naomi and making sure Rhode and Nathaniel were fed before leaving for the synagogue in the mornings.

Martha alternated with her sister in caring for Lazarus. His cough had deepened and started to produce blood. It wasn't something Martha wanted to tell anyone else because she knew it would terrify them, just as it terrified her. So the day before, she'd asked Benjamin to take a message to Jesus. When Benjamin had returned at dusk to report, he'd said the message had been delivered. If that was the case, then where was Jesus?

Did Jesus not think the illness was serious? She could only pray He would arrive today. But what if Benjamin had not made his message urgent? What if Jesus thought there was no hurry to return to Bethany?

The babe in her arms stirred, his sweet scent filling Martha with a pang of longing she couldn't explain. She resumed her humming, a sound that seemed to soothe the child. The babe had no name yet; Leah was waiting for Lazarus's recovery so they could choose a name together. 💙 💙

As Martha hummed, her thoughts turned to prayer again. It seemed all she did was pray during every waking hour. Lazarus was in grave danger, and they had no more resources to draw upon. All the teas, the poultices, the stews, and the incense burning had not brought Lazarus relief. And now he was coughing up blood.

Martha swayed in place with the child's round head tucked beneath her chin. Closing her eyes, she mouthed the words of yet another prayer, pleading for her brother's life to be spared.

A sound in the cooking room alerted Martha, and at first, she froze. But then she heard Mary's whisper.

"I can take him," Mary said, walking quietly into the gathering room.

Martha turned to see her sister, robe clutched around her, eyes widened.

"He's nearly asleep," Martha said. "I don't want to disturb him."

"You can't hold him all night," Mary said. "You're exhausted as well."

Martha offered a faint smile. "I couldn't sleep anyway."

Mary nodded, and she walked to the circle of cushions, where she settled onto one. "It's Lazarus, isn't it?"

Martha hesitated, then said, "Yes. He is worse."

Her sister didn't speak for a few moments as she sat with her knees drawn up to her chest, her chin atop her knees. Martha couldn't see her sister's expression from where she walked the floors, but the atmosphere in the room was solemn.

"We need to send for Jesus again," Mary whispered into the dimness. "Benjamin delivered the message, but Jesus still has not come. We've done everything any healer could do. Jesus is our last hope. He is the Master Healer, and He can save our brother's life."

Martha slowed her step. She'd witnessed firsthand the healing power Jesus held. Where was He? Why had He not arrived to help His friend? Martha exhaled, wishing her brother wasn't so ill, wishing everyone in the family was healthy.

"What more can we do?" Martha asked. "We've already sent one messenger."

Mary didn't answer for a moment and focused on her feet. "We need to send another person to let Jesus know that our brother is much worse. Jesus needs to know that He cannot delay. What about sending Horeb?"

It made sense, but Horeb was working doubly hard at the grove in Lazarus's absence. "Who would fill in for his work? We'd have to hire someone."

Martha didn't dare make such a move without Lazarus's permission, and he hadn't been coherent for days.

"Perhaps Horeb will have some ideas," Mary suggested. "Or Josiah could send a message with one of the caravans he trades with."

Martha continued her pacing, though her nephew was now sound asleep, his little body completely relaxed. "Perhaps. But if Benjamin couldn't bring Jesus here, how would complete strangers in a caravan? Besides, it might be days before word gets to Jesus and . . ." She cut herself off.

"And you don't think Lazarus has that long?" Mary whispered, her voice full of the emotion that had already hit Martha hard.

"I've never seen a man so ill," Martha said. "I've doubts that he'll survive if we don't see a miracle soon. A few hours ago . . ." Her voice broke, and she tried again. "A few hours ago, he coughed up blood."

Mary didn't move, didn't speak. Then she released a very slow breath. "What about Zachary? He could fetch Jesus. I could help watch over his flocks while he—"

"Lambing season is too close," Martha said. "Now is the very worst time for a shepherd to leave his flock."

Mary hung her head. "You're right. Who else in the village can be spared?"

No one, Martha thought. Every male had responsibilities to his land and his family. Unless someone was going on a journey to trade . . . but there was no one she could think of.

"We need to get the word out," Mary said. "I don't care how. Jesus needs to come."

The desperation in her tone matched the desperation in Martha's heart. "At dawn, we'll go and petition everyone we can. Perhaps someone will be able to help."

It was the best they could do, and both the sisters knew it. After Martha returned her sleeping nephew to a spot near Leah, Martha returned to the gathering room and lay down. She'd decided to sleep across the cushions so that she could listen for either Lazarus or his son. She was surprised that she slept at all, but when Mary gently shook her shoulder in the morning, Martha opened her eyes to early sunlight spilling into the room.

"I've given Lazarus some tea and renewed the poultice on his chest," Mary said in a hushed voice. "I've told Leah our plan, and she is grateful. Rhode and Nathaniel will help us make inquiries too."

Martha was impressed with her sister's resourcefulness. And in the next few moments, she headed to the cooking room and portioned out day-old bread for everyone. Before leaving the house, Martha crept into the chamber where Lazarus rested. His skin reminded her of the underbelly of a fish, cold and pale, and his breathing sounded labored. She knelt beside him, her heart aching at the sight of his struggling breath as it wheezed through his chest.

Whatever illness he had, it had ravaged his body. The circles beneath his eyes were violet, and his face appeared gaunt when it had normally been robust and fleshed out.

"We're going to find Jesus," Martha whispered, her voice thick. "And you'll be healed."

She needed to act because if she stayed here, she'd never be able to leave her brother's side.

Touching his arm, she continued. "We'll return as soon as possible. Rest and don't worry about anything." She rose to her feet and hurried out of the room, renewed urgency coursing through her.

It wasn't ideal to leave her ill brother behind and Leah with her new babe, but hopefully they could find someone quickly.

Mary waited outside in the courtyard with their nephews, and within a few moments, they had a plan put together of which houses to visit. Martha walked with Rhode, and they headed to the first house.

Eunice answered the door, her brows raised at the early-morning intrusion. Thankfully, it didn't appear that they'd awakened the woman. Her husband, David, came to the door and listened as Rhode told him about Lazarus and the hope to take a message to Jesus. Rhode's voice cracked more than once as he spoke, and Martha's heart tore just a little bit more.

"Jesus is a nomad," David said, his fingers combing through his beard. "There is no way we could track Him down, not even if we got a group of soldiers involved." He looked from Martha to Rhode. "I'm sorry, son. It is a difficult time of year to leave flocks and field planting. Who knows how long it would take to locate—"

"There must be a way," Martha interrupted. "A messenger, perhaps? I would pay whatever the cost."

David shook his head. "Where would you send a messenger? Which direction?"

Neither Martha nor Rhode had an answer, and she already felt a strong resistance coming from David.

"I am very sorry about Lazarus," David said, his tone gentler now.

Martha nodded. She didn't want sympathy. She had enough of that stored up. She wanted action and results.

"Thank you for your time," she told him, and after Rhode bade him farewell, they continued on. It was too early for the market to be up and running, but Martha hoped to find Josiah there anyway.

"Come on," she told Rhode. His entire demeanor was dejected. "Let's go see if anyone is at the market early." They hurried along the lanes, past the silent homes, until they reached the market square.

The market was a strange place to be when no one was around. She was right about Josiah, though. He'd already arrived and was warming his hands over a small cooking fire behind his cart.

"Rhode." Josiah straightened when he saw the pair of them approach. "Martha. Is everything all right?" Josiah knew firsthand how frantic Martha had been to try every concoction Josiah had ever heard about.

"It's Lazarus. He's getting worse, and we've tried everything," Martha said. "The poultices ease his pain, but now the cough has drawn blood."

Josiah winced.

Martha didn't wait for him to offer sympathies or condolences. She pressed on with her errand. "We need a messenger who can bring Jesus back to Bethany."

Josiah's eyes widened as he looked from Martha to Rhode. "Do you know where He is?"

"No," Martha said.

"We would pay you," Rhode broke in. "We could watch over your cart. I'd even make sales for you while you're gone. You can take one of my father's donkeys."

The desperation in Rhode's voice was unmistakable, and Josiah moved to the boy's side and set an arm about his shoulders. "If only I were ten years younger, my son," he said in a quiet voice. "But I'm afraid it's not safe for me to travel alone. There are thieves and bandits about, and I'm simply no match for them."

Rhode nodded, although Martha could see the disappointment etched on his face.

"What about Zachary?" Rhode asked.

Martha snapped her gaze to him. Did Rhode know Zachary?

"He could travel with you, protect you," Rhode continued. "I could watch over his flocks. Mary would help me."

Josiah glanced at Martha, then back again. "It's worth asking him."

Martha hated to even bring it up with Zachary. He was a shepherd, and the safe delivery of the lambs was his livelihood. Not only would Rhode have to make sure the sheep fared well, but he would also need to keep away any encroaching predators.

But she didn't have the heart to dissuade Rhode since a small bud of hope was growing inside her as well.

"Thank you, Josiah," Martha said. "We will go speak with Zachary."

Rhode's stride was full of purpose as they walked through the nearly silent village. The sky promised to be a clear blue once the sun rose fully, and now, the deep turquoise somehow made it seem impossible to believe that Lazarus lay dying back home.

"There's Nathaniel and Mary," Rhode said, pointing up ahead.

Sure enough, Mary and Nathaniel were coming out of a courtyard. It appeared they'd been turned down too.

Martha and Rhode caught up with them.

"I'm going to speak to Horeb," Mary said, determination in her voice.

"Mary—" Martha cut in.

"And you go speak with Zachary," Mary continued. "We've no choice now." She stopped in the road and faced the three of them. "If we want our brother to live, we need Jesus. And we need Him right away. This is no time to worry about flocks or fields or groves. We are talking about a human life here, and we need to appeal to those who care about our family."

Martha swallowed. "Very well. We'll go speak to Zachary, then meet you at the crossroads." She set off, Rhode at her side. What Zachary would say she didn't know, but she had to ask.

She thought of his gratitude when she'd come to help his daughter, Claudia. Now Martha was in need of a miracle.

Although the morning was early, Zachary wasn't inside his house. Smoke from the cooking fire behind the tent caught Martha's attention. She and Rhode walked the perimeter to find Zachary huddled near the fire, warming his hands as a pot of broth was heating up.

He straightened when he spotted them, and Martha noticed right away that he looked like he hadn't slept in a while. Her first thought was that Claudia had been ill again, but then she remembered that shepherds spent the nights with their flocks during the lambing season.

"What's going on?" Zachary said, not in a harsh tone but more concerned than anything. His brown eyes cut from Martha to Rhode, then back to Martha.

"It's Lazarus," Martha said. "He's . . ." She couldn't say the words, and she didn't know why. But for some reason, seeing Zachary and knowing what he'd been through with his wife and more recently his daughter made Martha wonder if she could bring this request to him.

"My father's dying," Rhode said in a stiff tone.

Zachary stepped forward and rested a hand on the boy's shoulder. "Josiah told me he was ailing. I am sorry. Your father is a good man."

Rhode nodded, and Martha wrapped an arm about Rhode's shoulders as he brushed tears from his face.

The three of them stood close together while Rhode gained control of his emotions. Martha's weren't far from surfacing.

"What can I do?" Zachary asked in a quiet voice.

In his eyes, she saw a man who was weary but a man who also had deep reserves of strength.

"We need someone to find Jesus and let Him know of our plight," Martha said in a rush. "We've been to everyone we can think of, but the planting season has started. And now the lambing season is upon us, so you are the last person—"

"I will go," Zachary said.

Rhode lifted his head and stared at Zachary.

Martha couldn't look away from his determined gaze.

"Perhaps Rhode can watch over my flocks for a few days," Zachary said. "He's a strong young man at thirteen years of age."

Rhode wiped at his cheeks again, then sniffled. "I will."

"Of course you will," Zachary said.

Martha couldn't believe what she was hearing. Was Zachary really offering . . .

"And your daughter can stay at our house, and Mary and Martha can take care of her," Rhode cut in. "Can she, Martha?"

"Yes, but—"

"It's settled," Zachary said. "I need only a few moments to gather some things for Claudia. Wait here."

Before Martha could come up with a reply, he'd disappeared inside the tent.

Rhode looked at Martha. "He's really going to help."

She nodded, biting her lip to keep her emotions in check. Zachary leaving his flocks this time of year had no parallel. The murmur of voices came from within—Zachary's lower tones and Claudia's higher-pitched ones.

Soon, father and daughter appeared, both carrying small bundles.

"Father says I can stay at your house while he goes on a journey," Claudia said, her face bright and her smile wide.

"Yes," Martha said. "You can help Naomi take care of her new brother."

"A babe?" Claudia echoed.

"Yes." She smiled, and her eyes connected with Zachary's for a brief moment.

"And your father can take our donkey on his journey so he can make better time," Rhode said as they set off along the road.

"Thank you," Zachary said.

Martha fell into step beside Zachary. "No, thank you. I can't tell you how much this means to me."

Zachary's nod was brief, but his eyes lingered on her face. "It is nothing."

Oh, but it was everything.

CHAPTER SIXTEEN
Mary

MARY PICKED HER WAY AROUND the olive trees with Nathaniel. Although it was still early in the morning, she could hear the thwack of an ax against wood as Horeb pruned. Limbs lay strewn about the ground, evidence of Horeb's hard work.

Lazarus had mentioned a time or two that Horeb didn't believe in wasting a single daylight hour. And that proved to be correct as Mary arrived at the scene of Horeb hard at work, even at this early hour, pruning the trees.

He didn't see them at first, and Mary hated to interrupt his diligent work, but he lifted his head as she approached.

Horeb's smile was quick and genuine the moment he saw her. But then his brows pulled down when he spotted Nathaniel, and Mary knew he was remembering Lazarus and realized she wouldn't be approaching so early in the morning if all was well.

Horeb propped his ax against an olive tree trunk, then brushed off his hands.

"What is it, Mary?" he asked, his voice low and warm yet wary. "Is it your brother?"

"Yes," she said, surprised that her voice was choked. "He is much worse, and we fear for his very life." She blinked rapidly, her eyes burning, her throat stinging.

"Father is not coherent," Nathaniel added. "He's coughing up blood now. The healer has tried everything, and so has Martha."

Horeb was at their sides in seconds. He didn't touch them, but Mary could feel his compassion as if he held her hand in his.

"We should ask the entire village to pray for him," he said. "Adonai will listen."

Horeb's faith had never stopped amazing Mary. "We need . . . we need someone to find Jesus and ask Him to come to Bethany."

Horeb didn't say anything for a moment, and Mary could practically see the thoughts flitting across his face. "I will go."

She hadn't even directly asked him, yet he was willing. "What about the grove?"

"I will work day and night when I return if I have to," he said in a fervent tone. "Can I take a donkey? If not, I can walk."

"You can take a donkey," Mary said, relief bubbling up in her chest.

Nathaniel grinned. "Let's go get the donkey now."

Mary's heart soared as they headed out of the grove and walked along the main road leading into the heart of the village. The morning was still early enough that the lanes and roads were empty.

"Mary," a boy called out, and she realized that Rhode, Martha, and Zachary were traveling in the same direction. Claudia was also with them.

Mary's group slowed to wait for them. "Horeb will go find Jesus," Mary said as soon as they were close enough.

"Then we will divide up and cover more ground," Zachary said, scanning the group.

"You've agreed too?" Mary said, wonder filling her. Horeb was very loyal to her brother, but for Zachary, it would be an even greater sacrifice.

"Father says I can stay at your house," Claudia piped up. "Martha says I can help with the new babe."

"And so you shall," Mary said, smiling down at the young girl.

"Come on," Rhode said. "Mother will be so happy with the news. Let's hurry."

Time was of the essence, and Mary hurried along with the group to their house. The sun finally spilled across the horizon as they turned onto the last lane. The soft gold rays bathed the houses they passed, making everything look brilliant and full of promise.

But as Mary opened the gate and headed across the courtyard, she heard someone crying, no, wailing. The first thought that went through her head was that the babe was awake again, but then she realized it wasn't an infant's cry; it was a woman's.

"Leah," Mary breathed, reaching for the door with trembling hands.

Martha was right beside her, and the two women rushed into the house.

Leah's cries echoed through the empty rooms, and Mary didn't know what to think. Was Leah ill? Had something happened to the child? To . . .

"Lazarus!" Mary called out, running after Martha, who'd taken off down the corridor leading to the bedchambers.

Mary stopped next to Martha, who hovered in the doorway. Leah was inside the boys' room, kneeling over Lazarus, clutching his clothing as she wailed.

"Lazarus," Mary cried out again, rushing into the room. She knelt on the other side of her brother's prostrate form. His skin was so pale that it was almost translucent. Mary stared at her brother's face, his closed eyes, his familiar cheeks, eyebrows, and beard. The lines about his eyes that deepened when he smiled.

He could very well be asleep, but Mary knew his spirit was gone. She *felt* the absence of it. She placed a hand on his chest. There was no rise and fall of breath, and his body was rigid and cool.

Leah continued to wail, and mixed in now were cries from other family members.

Mary gazed at the still form of her brother, hoping and praying for his chest to move, for his breath to return to his body. Lazarus gone . . . it was incomprehensible.

"No, no, no," Mary choked out. And then she couldn't look at her brother's body anymore. She couldn't be in the same room. She couldn't listen to the heart-piercing sorrow around her.

It was too late to save him.

Horeb and Zachary wouldn't be scouring the countryside now, looking for Jesus.

There would be no triumphant arrival and healing of her brother.

Mary moved out of the room, past Naomi clinging to her mother and Martha clutching the boys to her, past a stunned Horeb and Zachary in the corridor. Mary didn't stop until she reached the back courtyard and sank to her knees in the dirt of the reaped vegetable garden.

She couldn't breathe, couldn't think, couldn't comprehend.

Lazarus couldn't be dead. She'd never felt so abandoned, not even when each of her parents had died. She'd always had her brother, and he'd always promised to be there for her, to take care of her, even when she told him she wouldn't marry Isaac.

Mary closed her eyes, wanting this day to have never started. She wished that the sun had never risen, that she had not left the house when her brother had been taking his last breaths. He had a family, a wife, a new child.

After all the miracles they'd seen with Jesus's visit in Bethany and all the blessings in their lives, how could this happen? How could something so terrible and final happen?

Jesus had taught them about eternal life, and Mary knew it was true. She held on to that faith. But the pain coursing through her was unbearable.

Despite the walls separating her from the bedchamber where Lazarus lay, she could still hear the crying and keening. It wouldn't be long before the neighbors would arrive and join in.

She buried her face in her hands as she stayed kneeling in the dirt. She didn't notice the warming sun cutting through the chilly wind. She didn't hear the birds chirping their early spring songs. She felt nothing, saw nothing. All she could think about was that they'd been too late. They should have sent for Jesus days ago. He could have arrived by now, and her brother would have been healed.

"Mary," a gentle voice said as a hand rested on her shoulder.

She recognized Horeb's voice, but she didn't move or respond.

He knelt beside her, his hand still on her shoulder. "I am so very sorry."

Mary knew Horeb was sincere, but he'd only known Lazarus for a short time.

When Mary didn't respond, a few moments later, Horeb said, "He is in heaven now. He feels no more pain."

Mary knew the words were true, but she hated every single one of them. She couldn't speak; she didn't want to. Yet Horeb remained next to her.

She wasn't sobbing, but she kept her face buried in her hands. Her thoughts muddled together, and she couldn't sort any of them out.

The morning progressed, and still, she stayed outside. Horeb tried to coax her inside, but she only shook her head. Soon, he brought a rug and placed it over her shoulders. The morning passed, and she heard voices coming from the home. Visitors and mourners.

Around midday, Martha came into the courtyard. "Mary, come with me."

Mary didn't answer, couldn't answer.

Martha crouched before Mary and grasped her hands. "We must prepare our brother's body for burial," Martha said in a quiet but firm tone. "Leah is still recovering from childbirth, and it is our duty to do this last honor for Lazarus."

Mary looked into Martha's eyes. They were red-rimmed as they blinked back at her. It was clear that Martha had been crying as well.

"How can you do it?" Mary asked. "Continue on and stay on your feet despite the fact that our brother is dead? He's gone, Martha. Gone." Her voice broke, and she squeezed her eyes shut again. "What are we going to do? Rhode and Nathaniel are too young to take over the groves, and none of us women can go on trading journeys."

Martha only tightened her grasp. "I am relying on faith alone, Mary. I cannot think of tomorrow right now or next week or any day beyond that. All I know is that right now, today, you and I need to prepare our brother's body for burial. We will manage it somehow. We'll make it through the next hour together, then the one after that. But I need you, Mary. I lost a brother too. Please don't turn into yourself."

Mary clung to Martha's hands, then she let Martha draw her to her feet. Soon, the two women were embracing.

After a few moments, Mary took a deep, shuddering breath. Her sister needed her, and she needed her sister. She couldn't expect Leah to have the strength to prepare Lazarus's body for burial.

"What if I can't do it?" Mary whispered into Martha's hair.

"Then we will take a break," Martha said. "But we won't know until we try." She drew away and held Mary's gaze. "Come. Tamara has brought the oils, and Eunice has brought the burial linens."

"Already?" Mary said, blinking back the tears.

"You have been outside for some time," Martha said, no reprimand in her tone.

Mary tilted her head toward the sky to check the position of the sun. It was midafternoon. She had been out here for longer than she'd realized, not that her thoughts had been exactly rational in the first place.

"Horeb tried to get me to come in, but he eventually gave up."

"He didn't give up," Martha said. "He didn't want the villagers to speculate about the two of you."

Mary didn't have the emotional stamina to ponder what that might mean. But she knew she didn't want anything to mar her brother's or her family's reputation. Ever.

"Horeb is a good man," Mary murmured.

"Yes, he is," Martha said. "He offered to continue working without pay until we can figure out how to run the groves. We'll provide food for him, of course."

Mary nodded and swallowed past the swollenness of her throat. "Our brother knew how to pick his friends."

Martha's eyes brightened a fraction. "Yes, and we need to be grateful for our brother's legacy. He will be laid to rest before sundown, so we must make haste now."

Still, Mary hesitated. "Is the house full of people?"

"They didn't come to judge you, sister," Martha said quietly. "They're here to pay their respects to the family and offer condolences. Your failed betrothal with Isaac is a thing of the past."

Mary wanted to believe her sister, truly she did. But she hated to come face-to-face with one of the village gossipers. No matter what they said to her, she'd know what they were secretly thinking.

Martha grasped Mary's hand and led her toward the back entrance of the house.

"Leah has cleaned his prayer shawl," Martha said.

"She has done so much when she should be resting and grieving," Mary said—like she'd been resting and grieving, leaving all that work to everyone else.

"Keeping busy is keeping us from melting into puddles of despair," Martha said. "That will come soon enough."

With both reluctance and determination, Mary followed Martha into the house. A couple of women were in the cooking room, preparing a meal in hushed quiet.

Martha greeted them, but Mary only nodded. She didn't trust her voice to speak. In a few moments, she'd see her brother again. Her deceased brother, who would never walk or talk or laugh again.

Eunice and Tamara crossed to Mary and embraced her. She held on to each, drawing their strength to give her more courage to attend to her brother in a few moments.

"We are here for you, dear one," Tamara murmured as she pulled away.

"Thank you," Mary whispered.

Martha drew her along the corridor leading to the bedchamber. Mary stopped in the doorway as Martha continued into the room.

Lazarus lay upon the mat where he'd taken his last breath. Someone had placed a linen shroud over him, and the stillness of his form brought a fresh round of tears to Mary's eyes.

"Oh, Lazarus," Mary whispered. "Please let this be a horrible dream." But it was no dream. Her brother was beneath the shroud.

Martha extended her hand, and Mary took it. Together, the sisters approached the body and knelt on each side.

Martha slowly withdrew the shroud while Mary held her breath. Her brother's color was too pale, and she keenly felt his absence. But a calm had settled in the room since the other sounds throughout the house seemed far away now.

The two sisters began anointing Lazarus's head with oil, then cleansed his body with scented water, followed by more oil applications. The sweet fragrance filled the room, both soothing and edged with the pain in Mary's heart.

Martha had been right. Doing this last service for their brother was necessary and healing.

"Where are Leah and the children?" Mary whispered as they finished up.

"They've all been in her room," Martha said. "Naomi has cried herself to sleep, and the boys won't leave their mother's side."

Mary nodded, blinking rapidly. "I will go to them and offer my support. I spent too much time outside, selfish in my grief."

Martha reached over and took her hand. "Mary, we are all coping in the best way we can. No one criticizes you for taking time for yourself."

"Thank you," Mary said. "But if anyone taught me that I need to look beyond myself, it was Jesus and His parables of serving those in need. And my family taught me that love can carry us through anything. Leah and the children are in greater need than I am, and I should be focusing on them."

Martha's smile was soft. "You are a wonder, dear sister."

The two sisters rose from their task and embraced again.

Then Mary steeled herself for her next actions. Leaving the chamber, she walked to the one Leah and Lazarus had shared. Martha had been right; Naomi was asleep, curled next to her mother's side, and Rhode and Nathaniel also reclined close by. The entire family was on the platform bed.

Mary crossed the room and kissed and embraced Rhode, then Nathan. Next, she kissed Leah's cheek, then said, "I will take the babe for a while, and you can get your rest."

Leah smiled her gratitude.

Holding the precious child in her arms brought both tears to Mary's eyes and a sense of protection. She would help raise this little boy of her brother's, and she would do anything she could to make sure the family was provided for.

She walked the corridors, the babe cradled in her arms, as she thought about the contributions she could make. Maybe she could learn midwifery from Tamara. Or she could offer her services in embroidery and sell pieces at the market. It was really the only talent she excelled at. Or she could marry and ask her husband to help provide for her family. The men in the village who were in a position to take a wife had already heard about her rejection of Isaac. Although no one would say it to her face, she knew that her name was tainted. And she no longer had the protection and good reputation of Lazarus.

If only Jesus had come in time. If only . . .

CHAPTER SEVENTEEN
Martha

MARTHA HAD NOT VISITED YOSEF's grave site in weeks, not with the burdens of her family weighing upon her. Today, she only paused at Yosef's grave for a few moments. She had a much more recent family death to add to her sorrows.

She picked her way along the stony ground of the village graves. The air had turned warmer with the spring, bringing with it the fragrance of moist dirt and new flowers. The rocky hillside was peppered with green grass and budding flowers. A pretty sight if one's heart wasn't so heavy.

Now Lazarus had lain in the family tomb for four days. And here she sat upon a flat rock near the entrance. Beyond, deep in the earth, her brother had been laid to his final rest, joining both of her parents.

The morning was yet early, but the day promised to bring with it some heat. Four days . . . she could barely comprehend it. It had seemed that yesterday, she'd been forcing her brother to sip some tea and assuring him that all would be well.

And then that horrible moment of arriving home to hear Leah sobbing over her husband.

The experience of a wife grieving for her husband had been all too familiar, and Leah's pain had been Martha's pain.

Now, with three women unmarried living under the same roof, they would have to find a way to support themselves. Lazarus's land and wealth would pass to his two sons, but Rhode and Nathaniel were much too young to take on the responsibilities of grown men.

It would be up to the women, Martha knew. They would have to take over the care and the management of the grove. They would have to trust Horeb as their traveling tradesman. Martha was grateful that he was a good and honest man, but how long would he want to work under the tutelage of women and young boys?

Martha loosened her mantle, letting the warm spring breeze tug at her long locks as she untwisted her plaits.

No day in her life had ever been easy, so why should today or tomorrow be any different? As she let the warm breeze wash over her, she decided she'd only remain a few more moments, then return to the house and put her plan into action. Horeb was working day and night, and they needed to create a schedule where the women could help.

The sound of scuttling rocks caught her attention. She looked to see Zachary and Claudia trudging up the hillside. They hadn't noticed her yet, so Martha had the chance to observe them.

Zachary's head was lowered, and little Claudia clutched his hand. She seemed subdued as well. The pair paused, and Claudia stooped to pick a few of the newest wildflowers. Zachary gave his daughter a gentle smile and nodded.

Martha's heart clenched at the sight. The bond of their two-person family was unmistakable.

She hadn't spoken to Zachary since that terrible day he'd promised to drop everything to find Jesus. She'd wondered about him, how he and his daughter were faring in their tent at the edge of the fields. She supposed she should invite Claudia over soon, and the little girl could have some interactions with someone closer to her age.

But life had been so burdened as of late.

Tears burned her eyes as she thought of Lazarus and how much she simply missed him. If she erased all the burdens his death had brought upon the family, all that was left was the fact that she no longer had her dear brother. His opinions had always been so quick and sure. His laughter so ready. His generosity never withheld.

"Martha," a little girl's voice said.

She looked up again to see that she'd indeed been spotted.

Claudia released her father's hand and ran the last few steps to where Martha sat. She was surprised that Zachary didn't restrain his daughter like he had that first time she'd seen them at the grave site. Then again, they were no longer strangers.

Martha rose to her feet and smoothed her hair back, realizing she wasn't currently wearing her mantle. Zachary had stopped a few paces away. His dark eyes watched her, and it was as if he were trying to gauge how to act around her. Did he need to offer condolences again, or could they speak of other matters?

"Hello, Claudia," Martha said, surprised when the little girl wrapped her arms about Martha's legs.

"I told Father I hoped to find you here," Claudia said.

Martha didn't know what to say to that and looked to Zachary again. The edges of his mouth lifted as he gave a slight nod. Martha had the sudden urge to smile in return, but she held back.

"Look at the flowers I picked for Mother." Claudia held up her bunch of flowers.

"They're very pretty."

"Do you want some for your brother?" Claudia continued.

"Claudia . . ." Zachary started to say, a note of warning in his voice.

"I'd love some," Martha said. She gave Zachary the smallest of smiles, and he looked relieved.

"All right, Claudia," he said. "But don't go too far. I need to be able to see you at all times."

"I'll stay close," Claudia said cheerfully and scrambled away.

Martha watched her skipping among the rocks, bending every so often to pick a wildflower.

Zachary moved closer to Martha, but she kept her eyes on his daughter.

"There was a time," he said in a low tone, "I wondered if I'd have two of my family members buried here."

"Claudia is a strong little girl," Martha said.

"Thanks to your care and wisdom."

Martha continued to watch Claudia pick her way among some bigger rocks. Zachary had expressed his appreciation more than once, but this . . . this felt different. More personal somehow.

She felt his gaze upon her and no longer upon his daughter. She stole a glance at him.

"Martha, can I ask you a personal question?" he said.

Unbidden, her heart rate spiked. "Of course," she said, although she wasn't sure what he could possibly want to know.

"Why haven't you remarried?"

The question stunned her. Not that someone might ask but that *he* had asked. Perhaps he'd heard that she'd been widowed now for three years, and since she was still of childbearing age, it was a long while. But it wasn't long to Martha. Was Zachary simply curious, or was there more to his inquiry?

"You don't have to answer," he said.

She realized she'd taken several moments with her thoughts. "Yosef was a wonderful husband. My only regret is that no children were born to our union. I suppose I haven't stopped grieving and therefore have not considered remarriage.

With Lazarus and everything going on in our family, I've been so busy." She'd never spoken so many personal thoughts aloud to a person not related to her. Had she said too much?

"I understand your heartbreak and reluctance," Zachary said.

She knew he did because she'd been a witness of his sojourns to his wife's grave site. "I am sorry for your loss as well," she told him.

Claudia called out to her father, "Look!"

"Very nice," Zachary said, and Martha heard affection in his tone.

They said nothing for a few moments as Claudia continued her flower hunt, stopping every so often to pick another flower.

"You have many burdens, Martha," Zachary said. "And Claudia is fond of you."

Yes, Martha wanted to say, but she was confused at the direction this conversation was going. Zachary had been generous to offer to search for Jesus, and that had been repayment enough for her help with his daughter.

She looked up at Zachary to find his dark gaze upon her. This man was hardworking, gentle, and at times reminded her a little of Yosef because of his devoted character. But Zachary was not Yosef. Zachary was younger, and she'd seen him offer refuge to her sister, Mary. That act alone had quieted any of her straying thoughts.

"I am also sorry about your brother," Zachary said. "And I'm sorry he isn't here for me to speak to him about my desire to ask for your hand in marriage."

Martha stared at Zachary. "*My* hand?"

A crease formed between his brows. "I know that being a shepherd's wife isn't something you are used to, but the lambing season has proved fortuitous so far, and yesterday I spoke to Jeremiah the merchant about purchasing a lot from his property. I plan to start building in a few weeks."

Martha didn't know what to think. Zachary was offering *her* marriage? To care for his daughter, certainly, but there was so much more to a marriage than childcare. Marriage to Yosef had taught her that.

She wanted to understand the workings of his heart. He loved his daughter—that was undoubtable—and it seemed he would do anything to care for her. Including marrying Martha.

She looked away from the intensity in his expression, which she couldn't read. He didn't love her; that she knew, and she didn't expect that. Love grew from sacrifice and service in most marriages. A few couples, like Lazarus and Leah, had love from the beginning.

"Martha . . ." Zachary said, moving closer.

He didn't touch her, and she knew he was too respectful to violate propriety, but he was close enough to touch. This brought other memories to light, ones of intimacy shared with her husband. Marrying Zachary would surely open that part of her life again. He would want more children, expect more children.

"If there's someone I should ask permission from, I will," he said. "Otherwise, I am sure you know your own mind."

She should know her own mind, but she didn't.

Claudia was on her way back. In a few moments, their private conversation would be over.

"Why do you want to marry me, Zachary?" she whispered without looking at him.

He hesitated. Perhaps he was surprised at her bold question.

"Because I have hope."

She lifted her eyes to his, her heart starting a slow thump. This was not the answer she'd expected.

"Hope for what?"

He didn't shy away from her direct question and even more direct gaze.

"Hope that one day our hearts will heal and we can find happiness in each other."

Martha's eyes burned with tears. Oh, how she wanted to heal and find happiness. Was marrying Zachary the right answer, then? "My sister is yet unmarried, and she would not bring the burdens I have to a marriage."

The crease between Zachary's brows appeared again, then his brows lifted as if he'd just understood something. "You have never been a second choice, Martha." His hand brushed against hers so quickly and so lightly she almost doubted it happened at all. "It's my greatest hope that *you* will say yes."

The warm breeze stirred around them, lifting the scent of wildflowers with it. Buried deep inside, Martha had perhaps entertained the idea of remarrying someday. Zachary was hardworking, intriguing, direct in his conversation, and—dare she think it without betraying Yosef—Zachary's looks were pleasing. Those soulful, dark eyes of his, the sturdiness of his frame, the strong cut of his jaw, the gentle way he had with his daughter . . .

"Father!" Claudia called, her voice nearer than Martha had expected. "Horeb is coming up the hill."

Martha stepped back from Zachary immediately and turned to see that, indeed, Horeb was heading up the hill. And he was running.

Alarm shot through Martha. The look on the young man's face was not one of a man coming to pay his respects to a grave site but of someone with an urgent message.

"Horeb," Zachary said, grasping Claudia's hand and taking a few steps forward.

But Horeb's gaze was firmly upon Martha. "There is news," he said as he drew closer, his breathing labored from his running. He looked as if he hadn't slept in days, and his clothing was more ragged than usual.

"What news?" she asked, knowing her voice was trembling. She didn't know if she could take any more bad news. Was it Leah or one of her children? The new infant? Had someone fallen ill?

"Josiah was out watching for the next arriving caravan," Horeb said between gulps of air. "He said that he saw Jesus and His Apostles traveling toward our town a short time ago."

"Jesus is coming *here*?" Martha asked, her tone an octave higher. "To Bethany? Are you sure?"

"Josiah has the eyes of a hawk," Horeb said, gaining his composure. "Jesus is on His way."

Martha's heart soared. Jesus was coming . . . but . . . she looked from Horeb to Zachary, and she could see the same realization in his eyes. It was too late. Lazarus was already dead.

Her shoulders sagged, and she wanted to find a place to sit and cry. It was all too much. The hope of finding Jesus, then Lazarus's death, and now . . .

"My mantle," she whispered, looking about the ground. She located the embroidered cloth she'd left on the flat rock she'd sat upon. Then she twisted her hair back and tied the mantle about her head despite the shaking of her hands. "I must go to Him." If Jesus was truly coming to Bethany, He'd be mobbed again, and who knew when she could speak to Him.

"Where are you going?" Claudia asked, her voice small and innocent.

"To speak with Jesus," Martha said. Tears fell hot and fast. She didn't exactly know why she was crying, but she knew she was desperate to speak to Him.

She hurried down the hillside.

"Martha," Horeb called after her. "Wait."

But she didn't wait. She couldn't wait. Her feet had never moved so fast, and she ran along the outskirts of the village, not stopping for a moment, not even stopping to fetch her sister, Mary. Martha ran past the first fields and past the rock walls dividing property from the main road out of the village. She didn't stop when she saw a group of men approaching. Jesus was among them. This she was sure of before spotting Him.

As she neared, she finally slowed, her heart and breathing quickened. She needed to be able to speak to Jesus and not become a crying mess. Breathing in and out, she readjusted her mantle about her hair.

The men stopped as she approached, and she saw the recognition in their eyes. When she met Jesus's gaze, her chest burned with emotion. She wouldn't cry, though. She wouldn't beg. But the words tumbled out after Jesus greeted her.

"Lazarus is dead," she said, a sob threatening to escape despite her resolve. "Lord, if thou had been here, my brother wouldn't have died."

Jesus's gaze didn't waver from hers, and she continued. "But I know that, even now, whatsoever a person asks of God, God has the power to grant it."

The Lord's expression was gentle, knowing, and full of wisdom. "Thy brother shall rise again."

Yes, of course he would rise upon Resurrection. It had been only one small comfort, but he was gone now, and their entire lives had changed. She glanced at the Apostles, who had also gathered around. Their expressions were solemn and full of compassion.

"I know that Lazarus will rise again in the Resurrection at the last day," she said at last. She wanted Jesus to know that she'd learned His teachings; she hadn't forgotten them.

Jesus moved closer, His tone gentle as He said, "I am the resurrection, and the life: he that believeth in me, though he were dead, yet shall he live: And whosoever liveth and believeth in me shall never die. Believest thou this?"

Yes, she could never deny her knowledge. "Yes, Lord, I believe that thou art the Christ, the Messiah, which should come into the world."

Despite knowing that Jesus's arrival was too late for her brother, Martha still felt gratitude flow through her. His compassionate gaze made her feel that He understood her sorrow, for Lazarus had been His friend too. Closer to the village, others had noticed the arrival of Jesus and His Apostles, and soon the crowds would gather. Jesus asked after Mary, and Martha told him, "She is yet at home. I came as soon as Horeb informed me you were on the road to the village."

Jesus asked that she bring Mary to meet Him before He entered the village and was faced with the crowds.

So Martha took her leave, hurrying back home. By the time she reached the courtyard, several of the village women were there already. They'd made a habit of showing up each morning and preparing food while offering words of consolation.

Although it was early yet, honey cakes were baking, and the smell of cooking porridge filled the rooms as Martha moved to the cooking area. Mary was sitting at the table, cradling their infant nephew in her arms. Leah must still be sleeping, which was a good thing.

Martha greeted the other women, then whispered to Mary, "Come with me."

But the other women overheard. "Has Jesus come at last?" one woman asked.

"Yes, the Master has arrived," Martha said in a hushed tone. "He has asked Mary to come so that He might offer condolences about our brother."

"Let me hand the babe to Leah, and then I will come." Mary walked into the corridor, and Martha had time to breathe for a moment.

When Mary returned, the women left the house together. Taking the back roads again, they hurried to just beyond the village borders, not wanting to alert the rest of the village. Jesus was sitting on the rock wall, surrounded by His Apostles. There seemed to be a discussion going on, but as soon as the women neared, Jesus rose to His feet to greet Mary.

Mary sank to her knees before Jesus. She clutched the hem of His robe and cried out, "Lord, if thou had been here when my brother was ill, he wouldn't have died."

The other women had remained behind Martha, but now, they sank to their knees, weeping and keening over the loss of Lazarus. Martha blinked back her own tears. She'd grieved over her brother, yet even on the fourth day since his passing, the wound was still deep and raw.

Her chest tightened, and she blinked against the burning in her eyes.

Jesus turned his gaze upon Martha. "Where have ye laid him?" He asked in a voice that was gentle yet rose above the sound of the crying.

Martha exhaled. "Lord, come and see."

The group followed Mary and Martha as they led the way to the burial site. More people in the village were alerted, and soon a crowd had gathered upon the hill of tombs.

Martha motioned toward the tomb site, then stood to the side. Jesus clasped His hands and bowed His head before the stone covering the underground cavern. Martha's emotions welled again as she saw the tears in Jesus's eyes.

He was grieving for her brother too.

Mary slipped next to Martha, and the two sisters linked arms.

The crowd increased, and those in the back murmured, asking what was going on. Comments filtered through the crowd, and Martha heard one person say, "See how He loved him."

Other voices rose above the others, although they were still hushed. An older woman said, "He has opened the eyes of the blind, so could He not have prevented Lazarus from dying?"

Martha's heart pinched. These had been her exact criticisms, but now that Jesus was here, and she saw how He wept, Martha no longer felt frustration. Sorrow, yes, but peace also. She pulled Mary, whose crying had softened, closer. Martha closed her eyes for a moment. Jesus was here, and all would be well. Somehow, some way, she and the women of her family would survive this setback.

When she opened her eyes again, she felt another's gaze upon her. She turned her head to see Zachary standing in the midst of the crowd, seemingly apart from the others. She'd not given him an answer, not yet. In this moment, she felt strangely connected to him, as if they had the same heart. Their shared experiences linked them in a way unlike any other. But did that mean she should accept his offer of marriage?

His dark eyes were upon her, filled with sympathy for her lost brother and empathy for their shared state. She knew he was still waiting for her answer, an answer she wasn't ready to give. Not now.

Jesus stepped closer to the stone, and His movement shifted Martha's attention back to Him. Jesus ran the tips of His fingers along the crevices of the rock, then said in a firm tone, "Take ye away the stone."

CHAPTER EIGHTEEN
Mary

MARY WIPED AT HER EYES as she leaned against her sister. Jesus had commanded that the stone be moved from her brother's grave. Was Jesus going to descend into the tomb? The murmurs of the crowd grew louder. Some were wondering why Jesus had returned to Bethany. Because of His great love for His lost friend?

"Lord," Martha said, capturing His attention.

Mary stilled, wondering what her sister was about to say.

"By this time he stinketh: for he hath been dead four days."

The murmuring in the crowd had returned, and Mary felt the curiosity of the crowd match her own.

Jesus looked at the sisters, his mouth curved into the barest of smiles. "Said I not unto thee, that, if thou wouldest believe, thou shouldest see the glory of God?"

"Yes," Martha whispered.

Jesus nodded, then motioned for His Apostles Simon, Peter, and Andrew to step forward. Next, Horeb and Zachary joined in. The men rolled away the stone, exposing the tomb's opening.

Mary stepped back on instinct. The darkness of the opening of the underground tomb sent a rash of goose pimples across her skin.

The crowd had gone absolutely silent, and even Mary found she was holding her breath. *me too!!!*

Jesus lifted his chin and gazed upward, toward the sky. In a soft voice, He said, "Father, I thank thee that thou hast heard me. And I knew that thou hearest me always: but because of the people which stand by I said it, that they may believe that thou hast sent me."

Mary felt tears form in her eyes, although she didn't know why.

No one in the crowd spoke as everyone's gaze stayed riveted on Jesus.

His next words sent a warm shiver through Mary.

"Lazarus, come forth," Jesus cried out in a loud voice. Surely all in the crowd and beyond had heard Him.

Mary gripped Martha's arm tighter. The slightest sound had caught her attention. Above the sound of the spring breeze weaving among the rocks and new plants on the hillside, Mary heard shuffling footsteps coming from inside the gaping tomb.

She couldn't move, couldn't breathe, as the footsteps grew closer and became more distinct. And then a man emerged from the dimness. But it wasn't any man; it was her brother.

Mary gasped, shock rippling through her.

Lazarus wore the grave clothes that the sisters themselves had dressed him in four days ago. A napkin covered most of his face, but his eyes were clear and alert. No longer was his body cold and still, but breathing and alive. Lazarus blinked against the morning light, as if he'd just awakened from a long night's sleep.

"Loose him, and let him go." Jesus's soft voice sounded in the stunned silence.

One of the Apostles stepped up to Lazarus and gently removed the napkin and bindings. With every piece of cloth drawn away, the murmur of the surrounding crowd grew.

"Lazarus," Mary whispered.

He looked at her, then smiled.

Nothing could have held her back as she ran to her brother. She stopped short, afraid to touch him, for if she did, maybe she'd find out she was dreaming and that he wasn't, in fact, risen from the dead. But he grasped her hands and pulled her into his arms. His body was warm, solid, breathing, and she clung to him. Her head rested against his chest, and she could both feel and hear the thump of his heart—the same heart that had stopped days ago.

And then another person pressed against them.

Martha.

"Lazarus," Martha cried out, and Mary's tears started again too.

Lazarus kissed the top of Mary's head, then drew away from both sisters. Tears were in his eyes, and his face was not one ravaged by illness but one of joy and good health. His countenance seemed to glow even brighter than the midday sun.

"My sisters," Lazarus murmured, keeping a hold of their hands. "It has been a long sleep."

"You were d-dead," Martha said. "We washed and anointed your body and dressed you in grave clothes. We walked with the procession and laid you inside the tomb."

Lazarus's gaze shifted from Martha's to Mary's.

"It is true," Mary said. "We laid you to rest four days ago."

Their brother's eyes filled with wonder and warmth. Beyond the sisters, the crowd was pressing closer.

"Are you real?" their neighbor Eunice asked. She reached a hand out to touch Lazarus's sleeve.

"I am real, and I am alive," Lazarus said. "I have been brought back from the dead. How was this possible?" And then he saw Jesus. Lazarus's face broke into a smile. "You came."

Jesus nodded, and Lazarus sank to his knees, bowing before Him. "Thou hast brought me back from the grave, Master. Thou hast restored me to my family."

After that, the villagers swarmed both Lazarus and Jesus. Some asked for blessings from Jesus while others just wanted to touch Lazarus to verify what their eyes were seeing.

Mary watched all the goings-on, wonder overflowing her heart. She didn't bother drying her tears. She sought out one of the members of the crowd—Horeb. He grinned at her, and Mary smiled back. Lazarus was risen, and all would be well.

It was hard to grasp, hard to comprehend.

Leah needs to know, Mary realized with a start. She turned to find Martha. "We must take the news to Leah." Leah hadn't met the days of her purification yet, which was forty days following the birth of a male child, so she hadn't been able to go out in public.

Some of the members of the crowd were already leaving, likely to share the news with others in the village. Mary would hate for Leah to find out and wonder if the news was true.

"I will go to her," Martha said.

"No, I will," Mary said. "I'll return soon, unless Lazarus beats me home." Martha smiled, and the sisters shared an embrace.

Then Mary was off, hurrying toward the home that would brim with joy and happiness once again. She found Leah reclining in the gathering room, holding her babe close.

"Rhode and Nathaniel heard that Jesus has returned to Bethany," Leah said as soon as Mary entered.

"Yes." Mary smiled broadly. "And I have the most wonderful news. Jesus has raised Lazarus from the dead."

Leah only stared at her, then finally, she whispered, "How can this be?"

Mary sank to her knees in front of Leah and grasped her free hand. "The Lord called him forth out of the grave, and he walked out of the tomb. He is completely whole and healthy."

Tears filled Leah's eyes, and her hand shook as she gripped Mary. "I must see him." Then Leah rose to her feet, moved to the front door, and opened it. "Where is my husband?"

Mary joined her in the front courtyard. It seemed all of the villagers were out of their houses, congregating in courtyards, speculating about the news circulating through the village.

"Is it true?" Tamara asked, coming along the lane in front of their home.

"It is true," Mary burst out before Leah could reply. "I was at the tomb when Jesus called forth Lazarus." She told Tamara all that she'd seen.

"Blessed be this day," Tamara said with tears in her eyes.

Two men passed by their house, and seeing one of them was Isaac, Mary drew back, not wanting to have to interact with him. There had been no words or interactions between Mary or any member of his family since the night of their failed betrothal.

But Isaac slowed with his companion, taking in the sight of the women in the courtyard.

"We've heard the news," Isaac said, his eyes landing on Mary, then moving to Leah and Tamara. "Is it true that Lazarus has risen from the dead?"

Out of the three women, only Mary had been the eyewitness. Yet her reply was reluctant. "It is true."

She turned then and hurried into the house on a pretend errand. No one needed to know that she couldn't bear to be in the presence of Isaac. She didn't want the dark feelings to return. Yet she hovered by the window, curious about what else Isaac might say.

"Congratulations on the birth of your new child," Isaac continued, obviously speaking to Leah.

Her mumbled reply wasn't decipherable, but then Isaac said, "Tell me of the time that Jesus was here before. The time when He spent hours inside your home. What sorts of things did He talk about?"

"He spoke to Mary and Martha," Leah said, her voice clearer now. "You would have to ask them. Or you can ask Lazarus."

Isaac paused, and Mary strained to listen. "There is talk that Jesus has broken many laws, both of the Sabbath and of the land."

"I don't know of such things," Leah said, her tone stiff.

Isaac merely gazed at her for a moment, then said, "I need to report this new development to the Pharisees."

Mary clenched her jaw as she listened to Isaac. The Pharisees had only caused trouble for Jesus and hampered His ministry. If Mary were more confident, she'd march into the courtyard and tell Isaac to forgo delivering the message. But she wanted nothing to do with him, and she knew that beseeching him would have no effect.

She'd insulted and rejected him. He would never listen to her.

When Isaac left, Mary rushed into the courtyard.

"We can't let him speak ill of Jesus," Mary said to Tamara and Leah.

Both women turned. "It is not our matter," Tamara said. "Please be calm. Lazarus is coming now, and we want his reunion to be joyful."

Both Mary and Leah looked down the lane.

Leah gasped. "It is him," she said in wonder, her voice breaking. "It's truly him."

Mary held out her hands for the babe, and Leah handed the child over, then rushed to meet her husband at the edge of the courtyard. The two embraced for a long moment, clinging to each other, Lazarus murmuring words of comfort that were indecipherable.

Villagers crowded into the courtyard, but Lazarus waved them off and said he would return after he spent some time with his family. Mary went inside with them, and while she held the babe, Lazarus greeted his sons and little Naomi, then told them all of the events.

Leah wouldn't release her husband's hand, and despite the number of people gathering outside the house, Lazarus seemed in no hurry to leave Leah's side.

Mary paced the gathering room, the babe in her arms, and soon the child slept. But still, Mary paced.

She kept an eye on the courtyard and the lane beyond. People were coming and going, forming small groups.

After a while, she handed the babe to Leah, who took the child into the bedchamber for a feeding. But Mary returned to her watch of the courtyard, and it wasn't long before Lazarus joined her. His hand rested on her shoulder, and she leaned into him. Her strong, solid, and living brother.

"What concerns you, Mary?" he asked in a quiet voice.

Mary didn't want to trouble her brother, but she couldn't get over what Isaac had said. She told her brother about the conversation and was both gratified and worried that he took it seriously.

"Jesus has likely left Bethany by now."

Mary straightened from her brother and looked up at him. "Already?" She'd assumed He was teaching and healing among the villagers. Perhaps He would come to their home for another meal.

"He has followers all over the country," Lazarus said. "On my way back home, there were many congratulations, but there were also . . . those who continue to speculate."

Mary frowned. "About what?"

"Threats have been made against Jesus's life," he said. "The Pharisees' murmurings and complaints have grown. Not only has He violated the laws of Moses over and over, they say, but He teaches of things that threaten the government."

Mary could only nod.

"More and more of His followers are calling him the King of the Jews," Lazarus said in a lowered tone. "Word has traveled far and wide, and that doesn't endear Him to any members of our Roman government. There are some who want him brought to trial to have his fate decided once and for all."

"A trial for what?" Mary asked with growing horror. "He's harmed no one, committed no crimes. Just because His followers say things, that doesn't mean Jesus is claiming them for Himself."

"I agree, but the naysayers want Him tried for sedition," Lazarus said. "It's a capital crime against Rome and our governor, Pontius Pilate, to declare yourself as king. Even if Jesus hasn't said the words, His followers have."

Mary pressed her lips together. She knew this, but it was all hard to comprehend. She'd sat at Jesus's feet and listened to His gentle voice teach in a loving manner. "Perhaps enough time will pass, and the threats will diminish."

Lazarus didn't answer for a moment, and when he next looked at Mary, she saw the regret in his eyes.

"What is it?" Mary asked, wondering if she wanted to know more bad news.

"There are those in our village," Lazarus said in a slow voice, "who support the criticisms made by the high priest Joseph ben Caiaphas. Not only has Caiaphas demanded a trial, but his supporters would have no problem enacting capital punishment. Jesus was told by His Apostles that coming to Bethany would put Him in danger of stoning."

Mary stared at her brother. "Stoning? *Here*? Who would do such a thing?"

Lazarus exhaled. "There are a growing number who support Caiaphas."

"Even the Jews?"

"Yes," he said, and the confirmation rocked through Mary's heart.

"And to think I might have married one of them," she whispered.

"Isaac?" Lazarus said.

"I have no proof, but his words were unmistakable." She blinked back the tears forming in her eyes. "Do you think . . . do you think it was a blessing that I could not bring myself to marry Isaac?"

Lazarus turned to the window. People had moved on, but now Horeb entered the courtyard. "It is very possible, sister."

Horeb's knock on their front door was quiet, yet it sent a thudding through Mary.

She moved out of the room before Lazarus opened the door and welcomed Horeb. From the cooking room, she could hear their joyful greeting, and Mary had to smile. Despite the distressing news about the threats against Jesus and the possible impending trial, she had much to rejoice in. Her brother's life had been restored, and all was well in their small household.

Mary didn't get to work as she'd planned but instead remained still and listened to the conversation between the men. She didn't exactly consider it confidential since Lazarus would have moved out of the house if that was supposed to be the case.

"He has left Bethany," Horeb said.

"It is as I thought," Lazarus said. "Where is He going?"

"Ephraim," Horeb said. "But He only told me, so it's not information we can share with anyone else. Passover is approaching, and He wants to stay away from Jerusalem."

Mary knew that many would travel to Jerusalem for Passover early in order to purify themselves. Those who lived more than seventeen miles away from Jerusalem would have to go through a purification process at the temple.

"It will not be safe if He goes to Jerusalem," Lazarus said, echoing Mary's thoughts.

"If He does not show, it will be a big statement that will only strengthen the opposition of the Pharisees against Him," Horeb said. "But if He does show, He will put Himself in the direct path of the chief priests and the high priest."

"Caiaphas."

"Yes."

Mary closed her eyes, bringing her hands to her heart. All of her reading and studying had taught her the prophecies of Jesus's birth. It had also taught her the prophecies about His death. She knew He would go to Jerusalem eventually. *Stay in Ephraim*, she wanted to tell Jesus.

Even if she could get a message to Him, Jesus had a mission in this life. He'd brought the living waters to the people of her country to heal every wound and every stripe.

Mary turned from the conversation on the other side of the wall and made her way through the cooking room. She went out the back door and settled on a low bench in the courtyard. For a few moments, here, she could sit undisturbed, although her mind was far from rest.

Jesus's death was already prophesied, and there was nothing she could do to stop it.

CHAPTER NINETEEN
Martha

MARTHA HAD NOT SEEN OR spoken to Zachary for two days, not since their encounter at the burial site when he'd asked her to be his wife. She tried not to think about it because even though she'd been caught off guard, she'd now had time to entertain the idea. And she found it favorable.

Yes, she knew Zachary would not love her the same or as much as he seemed to have loved his first wife. And perhaps the same could be said of her. Would she be able to love another man, care for him with her whole heart, in the way she had for her first husband, Yosef? Martha couldn't see how.

But time had moved on, and the edges of her sorrow had softened.

Perhaps it was because of the miracle of her brother's life and the new hope that Jesus had brought, but Martha had felt a weight lift. One she hadn't realized she'd been carrying.

"Martha," Mary called through the narrow opening of her bedchamber door.

Mary had been an early riser as of late. It was as if the reemergence of their brother had stoked a new fire within her. They'd also had many visitors to their home, often from dawn until dusk. People had traveled from different villages, curious to see the man Lazarus who'd risen from the dead.

"I'm awake," Martha said. In fact, she'd been awake since before dawn, but she hadn't prepared for the day yet or left her bedchamber. "Come in." She sat up in her bed as Mary walked into the room, a satchel over her shoulder.

"Lazarus has had some news about Jesus."

This brought Martha to full awareness. "So early in the morning?"

"It seems the Pharisees and their allies do not sleep," Mary continued, sitting on the edge of the platform bed. She set the satchel next to her. "Isaac returned from Jerusalem early this morning, and he's already reported his news. Caiaphas has increased his accusations, and Jesus is on His way to Jerusalem."

"What?" Martha asked, her mind reeling. "Surely Jesus knows there is danger to His life there. Even if it is the Passover, Jesus could be tried and convicted."

Mary looked down at the hands clasped in her lap. "He knows. He also knows that a trial will be a death sentence. Don't you see, Martha? He will be the Passover itself. On the road to Jerusalem, He prophesied of His own death."

Martha had no answer. She could not comprehend such a thing. "He must not go to Jerusalem, then. Lazarus should warn Him."

Mary stared at Martha. "Don't you see? The death of Jesus has been foretold for centuries." She brought out a scroll from the satchel next to her on the bed. "Listen to what Zechariah said: 'Rejoice greatly, O daughter of Zion; shout, O daughter of Jerusalem: behold, thy King cometh unto thee: he is just, and having salvation; lowly, and riding upon an ass, and upon a colt the foal of an ass.'"

"What does it mean?" Martha asked, not having studied or learned as Mary had.

"The people will rejoice that Jesus is returning to Jerusalem," Mary said. "The ancient prophet Zechariah speaks about how the Messiah would be a priest, governor, and humble king. But He would also return to Jerusalem in triumph."

"So this is good news?" Martha prompted.

Mary again looked down at her clasped hands. She didn't answer for a moment, and when she lifted her head, tears shone in her eyes. "The Messiah will be rejected by His own people. There are too many who are against Him, and they have a powerful voice led by Caiaphas."

Martha exhaled. "Is there a prophecy about that too?"

Mary nodded and withdrew a much older scroll. She smoothed it open. "The prophet Isaiah said, 'Who hath believed our report? and to whom is the arm of the Lord revealed? . . . He is despised and rejected of men; a man of sorrows, and acquainted with grief: and we hid as it were our faces from him; he was despised, and we esteemed him not.'"

Martha had heard the prophesies of Isaiah discussed by men, including Yosef and Lazarus. But it had never felt so personal until now. "Perhaps these things have already come to pass. We know that His life has already been in danger. Maybe He won't be brought to trial."

"No," Mary said, her voice a whisper. "He will be betrayed by one of His followers. The psalms of David are twofold." She searched in her satchel until she found the scroll she was looking for. "'Yea, mine own familiar friend, in whom I trusted, which did eat of my bread, hath lifted up his heel against me.'" She took a breath. "And then again, in a later psalm by David, he said,

'For it was not an enemy that reproached me; then I could have borne it: neither was it he that hated me that did magnify himself against me; then I would have hid myself from him: But it was thou, a man mine equal, my guide, and mine acquaintance.'"

Martha thought of the Apostles she'd met. Could it be one of them? The thought was devastating. All of the Apostles had healed and blessed the sick and aided Jesus in teaching the new way. "How can this be? His Apostles have seen His miracles firsthand. They cannot deny what they have seen. Nor can they resent Him."

"It is unfathomable," Mary agreed.

The two sisters sat in silence for several moments as the rising sun's rays tracked across the bedchamber. Then Mary pulled out another scroll from her satchel. This one was not ancient but looked as if it was something Mary used to write on. "This is the message Lazarus received—the words of Jesus spoken to His Apostles and passed along to His followers."

"What does it say?"

Mary began to read. "'Behold, we go up to Jerusalem; and the Son of man shall be betrayed unto the chief priests and unto the scribes, and they shall condemn him to death.'" Her voice broke.

Martha closed her eyes. How could Jesus return to Jerusalem if He knew what awaited Him?

"'And shall deliver him to the Gentiles to mock, and to scourge, and to crucify him.'" Mary's voice trembled with emotion as she continued. "'And the third day he shall rise again.'"

"Crucify," Martha whispered. It was a slow and horrible death, one reserved for criminals when the government wanted to warn others against the same crimes. The convicted criminal would hang on the cross with no food or water until starvation or lack of breath took his life. "And then He will rise again on the third day?"

Mary wiped at her eyes. "Yes."

Martha released another slow breath. "Is there nothing we can do for Him?"

"Pray," Mary said, her tone resigned.

"I understand that the prophesies must come to pass," Martha said, feeling an urgency build within her. "But Jesus is a young man, only in His third decade. Surely there is much more for Him to do upon the earth."

Mary carefully set all of her scrolls into her satchel, then stood. "This is why I have come to your bedchamber this morning, to explain all that I know. I have only told you partial information so far."

Martha frowned. "What do you mean, sister?"

"I can't say if Jesus would have lived longer upon the earth if He hadn't raised our brother from the dead. He has performed a feat only Divinity can perform. Our brother has received word that Jesus's followers have multiplied." She crossed to the window that overlooked the lane below. "Look outside."

"What is it?" Martha climbed out of bed and joined her sister at the window. Below, a line of people stood outside their gate. Some were sitting; others looked as if they'd been there all night with their bundles and sleeping mats. How had she not seen them last night? And then she thought of how tired she'd been after two days of rejoicing and reorienting her life once again. "Who are they?"

"They want to see Lazarus," Mary said. "They want to witness for themselves the miracle of Jesus."

Martha shouldn't be surprised, but she was. As she gazed down at the line of people, another man appeared, moving at a quick pace. It took only a moment for her to recognize Horeb.

He spoke to those in line and seemed to be ushering them away from the house. As the sisters watched, one by one, the people took up their bundles and left.

"He's making them leave," Mary said on an exhale. "Is there nothing that man cannot do?"

Martha saw the faint color on her sister's cheeks. "He is a good man and a good employee for Lazarus."

"Yes, he is," Mary said.

The look they shared said what words couldn't—they understood each other.

"He is young," Mary said. "Young yet to take on a wife and the responsibilities of a family."

Martha smiled gently and grasped her sister's hand. "The weeks and months will pass, and soon he won't be as young."

Mary returned the smile, then gave a soft laugh. "Am I that transparent?"

"Only to me," Martha said, although she would be surprised if Lazarus and Leah hadn't noticed Mary's keen interest in Horeb.

It might take months, even a year or more, for Horeb to be established in Bethany and to be making a living beyond that of a common laborer at the grove.

Mary turned back to the window, and so did Martha. The line of people had now scattered, although Horeb remained at the gate to the courtyard as if he were a sentinel.

"Does the man never sleep?" Martha marveled.

"I don't think so," Mary said, both amusement and respect in her tone. "The day our brother aided Horeb was a blessed day indeed."

Martha couldn't agree more. Below, Horeb's attention had been caught by something, and Martha followed the direction of his gaze.

"What is it?" Mary murmured.

"It's a . . . mob." Martha stared at the approaching men. There were at least a dozen of them, and several carried spears and other weapons of war. She didn't recognize any of them at first, and then . . . she saw Isaac.

"Isaac," Mary said at the same time Martha realized who it was.

"He's—"

Isaac pushed Horeb against the gate in a threatening manner. Mary screamed, and Martha gasped in horror.

Horeb shouted for Isaac to leave the property, his voice echoing through the courtyard and reaching the upper-floor bedchamber, but Isaac didn't seem to be backing off.

"Lazarus," Mary cried out. "We must tell him."

"Where is he?" Martha asked, grabbing her robe and rushing out of the room. She fled down the corridor and stopped at the top of the staircase.

Lazarus was leading Leah and the children up the stairs toward her.

"Stay up here," Lazarus said to Martha. "I will send someone to guard the staircase until the frenzy dies down."

Martha stepped aside as Leah rushed past her with her children, and before Lazarus could head back down the stairs, Martha grasped his arm. "What is happening, brother? Why are Isaac and those men trying to get into our courtyard?"

Lazarus held her stare, his brown eyes intent on hers, but she saw his indecision, as if he didn't want to tell her something he'd regret.

"There's a declaration from the chief priests," Lazarus said in a whispered tone.

"A declaration about what?" Martha pressed. Her brother had pulled from her grasp and gone down a step. "Tell me."

"The news of my miracle has spread far and wide," he said, his tone still hushed. "The chief priests are blaming me for the number of followers who are supporting Jesus. And the chief priests want me . . . . dead."

Martha stared at her brother, stunned. "No."

He nodded, regret filling his eyes. "All of Jerusalem is in an uproar," he said. "Caiaphas has doubled his efforts, and when Jesus arrives in Jerusalem, it will be the beginning of the end."

Martha closed her eyes. "So what Mary said is true." Not that she'd doubted, but hearing her brother confirm it made it all the more real. She opened her eyes to find her brother's gaze stoic.

"It is true," Lazarus said.

"What does Isaac want with you?" she whispered.

"He wants to arrest me and take me to Jerusalem."

Martha covered her mouth. "What will you do?"

"I've a plan to evade Isaac, but he won't be the only one seeking my capture."

Martha's stomach felt like she'd swallowed pebbles. How could this be happening? After all the miracles and blessings? Her attention shifted to the sound of footsteps coming up the stairs. When the dark, curly hair of Zachary appeared, Martha started.

"Zachary," she breathed.

He held Claudia's hand in one of his, and in the other, he gripped a spear. Across his chest was slung a bow.

"Go to Martha," Zachary said, releasing his daughter's hand. Claudia scurried up the last few steps.

Before Martha could say anything, Zachary said to Lazarus, "I'll guard the stairs. You escape out the back way. No one will get past me."

Lazarus clapped a hand on Zachary's shoulder. "Thank you, my friend." Then he glanced back at Martha. "Be safe, dear sister."

She watched him head down the stairs, taking all her questions and doubts with him. Claudia slipped a hand into Martha's, and Martha looked down at the young girl. Her wide, trusting eyes looked up at Martha.

"Father said I can play with Naomi, but we have to be very, very quiet."

Martha swallowed. "Of course you may." She turned to Zachary. "Why are you here?"

His dark eyes were a deep well she couldn't see the end of. "Just as I told your brother—for protection."

"Putting yourself in this position only sets you in the middle of it," Martha said.

Zachary didn't waver. "I know."

Martha didn't have a reply to that. She moved up a step and reached the landing, still holding Claudia's hand.

Zachary gave her the slightest nod.

Martha nodded right back, then turned. Walking down the corridor, firmly holding Claudia's hand, Martha found herself overwhelmed once again by Zachary's generosity.

As soon as Claudia saw Naomi, the two girls found their own corner of the room to play in. Martha couldn't sit still, though. Worries plagued her mind. She paced the room, then paced the corridor outside. When she heard footsteps on the floor below, she went to the top of the stairs again.

Zachary passed by. He glanced up, and his steps slowed.

"Is everything all right up there?" he asked, concern in his dark eyes.

"All is well," Martha said.

But she didn't leave the landing, and Zachary didn't move either. Their gazes remained locked, and Martha sensed Zachary wanted to say something, but for some reason he was hesitant.

"If there's anything you need in the cooking room, help yourself," she said. "I could come down and prepare a meal—"

"No," Zachary said, lifting his hand. "That's not it."

She waited as he looked down, then back up at her, his eyes more intense now. "I know this is not the ideal time, and maybe with the events such as they are, there may not be an ideal time. But I have something to ask you, Martha."

The softness of her name on his lips tugged at something deep inside her.

"You are a woman unlike any other," he said. "And I would be honored—honored if you'd consider becoming my wife."

Martha heard the words, but she wasn't sure she could comprehend them. Her brother was alive now, and the family was not as desperate as they had been without their patriarch and protector. She didn't want to marry a man who pitied her.

"Zachary, with the return of Lazarus, you no longer need to rescue me."

His brows lifted, and his mouth opened. No words came out.

"I will be fine, and I want you to know that you and your daughter will always be dear to me."

"Martha." Zachary moved up a step. "I am not asking you out of pity or any sense of duty. I am asking you to be my wife because I want to spend the rest of my life with you."

Martha's eyes burned at his declaration.

Zachary hadn't moved, but his demeanor made her feel as if he were standing right in front of her.

"If you are in agreement, I would like to speak to your brother and ask for his permission." His smile was faint, hopeful. "*If* I have your permission to do so."

The gentleness and sincerity of his tone pushed something in Martha's heart aside, and she felt her own smile begin. "You have my permission."

CHAPTER TWENTY
Mary

THE DAY CRAWLED BY AS Mary kept watch out the window. She helped with the children, held the babe, played with Naomi and Claudia, and went over the prophesies with Rhode and Nathaniel. But it was Martha who would fetch food from the cooking room, in company with Zachary, then bring it back to the bedchamber where the women and children were camping out until Isaac and his crew gave up trying to find Lazarus.

Mary had no idea where her brother had gone. He'd tasked Horeb with more responsibility, so the man was overseeing the operations of the groves as well as monitoring the laborers. Mary was pretty sure the man hadn't slept much, if at all. But her greater worry was the division happening in the village: those who were followers of Jesus and those who wanted Him brought to trial for sedition.

From the window, Mary watched Horeb tirelessly turn people away from their home. He didn't waver in his diligence, and Mary found herself wishing more than once that he was older and more established—and in search of a wife.

Her face heated at the thought, and she then turned from the window to distract herself with another task. Her brother's life was in danger, and Zachary and Horeb were taking turns stationing themselves at the house to protect them. She should remain focused.

As the sun set and the day shifted into night, Martha went to the cooking room to retrieve food so they could have some semblance of a meal. When she returned, Martha seemed more cheerful and her countenance brighter, although nothing about their situation had changed.

They lit oil lamps as the night deepened. Mary wasn't sure how they'd all sleep in the same bedchamber with the babe's habit of waking more than once during the night, but perhaps they could occupy the third-level rooms as well.

Martha's voice rose and fell with a story she was telling the younger girls; Rhode and Nathaniel went over their lessons; and Leah held her sleeping babe in her arms. All was peaceful inside the home of Lazarus. If only he were home, safe and sound.

Mary paced the room, keeping her body and mind active so that her thoughts wouldn't turn too worrisome. When someone knocked on the door, Mary was the closest, so she opened it, fully expecting to see Zachary.

Instead, it was Horeb carrying an oil lamp that cast a warm glow over his face. He did a quick scan of her face before he asked, "Are you all right?"

"Yes," she said. "Have you heard from Lazarus?"

Horeb shook his head and looked past Mary to Leah, who soon joined them.

"Both Zachary and I will station ourselves outside tonight in case anyone else comes by," he told Leah. "Otherwise, you will have use of the rest of the house."

Leah nodded. "Thank you, Horeb. We appreciate your protection."

"There isn't much I wouldn't do for Lazarus and his family." He smiled at Leah, then his smile shifted to Mary.

His smiles always made her feel like smiling back, even at times like this, when her brother was in hiding and Jesus was in danger of losing His life.

"We are so grateful for your help," Martha said, joining them at the doorway.

Horeb nodded to Martha, then his gaze shifted between the three women. "I have some news. You cannot tell your neighbors, though."

"Of course not," Mary said immediately.

"Jesus has arrived at Simon the leper's home in Bethany. He will stay the night there, and I'm not sure about His plans for tomorrow."

Mary's chest expanded with both anticipation and sorrow. Would she be able to see Jesus one more time? "And then He goes to Jerusalem?"

Horeb gave a solemn nod. "That is what I've heard."

Mary turned away then. She had to see Jesus. Somehow. She would go to Simon's house in the morning, she decided. Looking at Martha, Mary saw the understanding in her eyes; they would go together.

That night, the family returned to their own bedchambers to sleep. Mary took a final look outside, seeing Horeb standing guard at the gate, true to his word. She climbed onto the bed and pulled the covers over her. She felt like she'd been praying all day for her brother's safety, but she continued to pray in her heart and finally fell asleep.

Hours later, when she awakened, she was grateful to see that dawn was approaching and the sky was already softening to violet. A new day. She hurried through dressing and headed down the stairs to find Martha already awake, preparing the morning meal.

"Did you sleep?" Mary asked her sister.

"A little," Martha said. "I am assuming you still want to go to Simon's home to visit Jesus?"

"Yes," Mary said. "Can we?"

Martha's smile was tender. "We will go. Eunice and Phebe are there to help with the meal. I would like to help too. And you, my dear sister, might speak to Him."

Mary knew how deep this kindness went. "Thank you."

Martha nodded. "Also, I've taken food to Zachary and Horeb. They won't leave their posts until Lazarus has returned. And even then, they said they might have to still protect him. We have another protector too. Josiah is also here. His cart is parked behind the house, and he is taking shifts with Horeb and Zachary."

"These men have been generous to our family," Mary said as she took over the stirring of porridge from Martha. "How long will our brother be in hiding?"

"I don't know," Martha said. "Zachary says it might be wise for him to remain in hiding until after Jesus's trial."

"You mean when Jesus is sentenced to death, the chief priests won't be too worried about our brother anymore?"

Martha set her hand on Mary's shoulder. "I hate this too."

Mary nodded, then turned her attention to the pot she stirred. She wished today was a different day, one before Lazarus's illness. The day when she and Martha sat at Jesus's feet and learned.

And now, she hoped to see Him today, to pay her respects for the last time. Her eyes burned with emotion, and the sun wasn't even up yet.

"Mary," Martha said in a soft voice. "You understand more than most the prophecies of the Messiah's birth and life and death. We are blessed to be witnesses of His goodness. We are blessed to have learned from Him personally."

"Yes," Mary said, wiping at her eyes, then continuing her stirring. "I just wish the way was easier. I don't want to think of what He might go through and the unfairness of it all."

Martha nodded. "Zachary told me this morning that since Passover season in Jerusalem will be packed with visitors, the trial will be after Passover, when Caiaphas doesn't have to contend with so many loyal followers."

Mary noticed the faint blush on her sister's cheeks when she spoke of Zachary. "Any delay is welcome," she mused, then hesitated. "Martha . . . do you and Zachary have a special understanding?"

Martha's brows shot up, but her blush deepened. "What do you mean?"

Mary smiled. "You know what I mean. Are you sweet on him?"

Setting her hands on her hips, Martha said, "No such thing. I was a married woman, and he was—"

"A married man," Mary cut in with a laugh. "Yes, I know. You are both widowed, dear sister. There's no reason each of you shouldn't marry again and no reason it shouldn't be to each other."

Martha's lips pursed, then tugged upward into a smile. "If I tell you something, do you promise to keep it silent?"

Mary's pulse leapt. "Yes, of course."

"Zachary . . . asked me to become his wife," Martha whispered, even though they were alone. "It was before Jesus came to Bethany and healed our brother. So I thought with the return of Lazarus that Zachary would change his mind. I mean . . . I thought he was offering out of the generosity and pity—"

"Martha—"

"I know." Martha held up her hand. "I had many worries at the time, and Zachary's inquiry only scrambled everything together even more. But . . . last night when I was pacing the floor above, I heard Zachary below. And he renewed his inquiry."

Mary found she was holding her breath. "What did you say?"

Martha closed her eyes for a second, then shook her head. She opened her eyes. "Something foolish about my brother being alive again. And that surely he didn't need to rescue me any longer."

Mary stared at her sister. "Heavens."

"Zachary looked offended," Martha said. "And I guess he had the right to be. He said he wasn't trying to rescue me."

Mary couldn't stop her growing smile. "And what did you reply, sister?"

"I told him . . ." She took a deep breath, but she was smiling. "I told him he had my permission to speak to my brother."

"Oh, Martha." Mary threw her arms about her sister's neck. "I can't believe it. I mean, I can, but I'm so happy for you."

Martha laughed and pulled her close. "I can't believe it either."

Footsteps sounded, and Nathaniel and Rhode arrived, looking like two hungry boys. While Martha made sure they had enough to eat, Mary slipped back up the stairs to grab her mantle from the bedchamber. She wrapped it about her hair, then secured it and returned to the cooking room.

Martha looked up as Mary came in, and soon they were ready after admonishing the boys to listen for their mother in case she needed help with the babe.

They exited the back door only to find Horeb there, feeding the goats. Josiah was lying on a mat under his cart, asleep.

"You don't have to do our chores, Horeb," Mary said in a quiet voice so as not to disturb Josiah. "My brother has tasked you so much already with the groves."

He turned with a smile, but that didn't hide the circles beneath his eyes and the exhaustion spread across his face. "Feeding the goats is a small matter. Besides, I hope to one day be more than a business partner with Lazarus."

Mary knew she was on the brink of blushing. She shouldn't assume that he meant . . . When she glanced at her sister, Martha's smile was coy.

A scuffle from beneath Josiah's cart caught her attention, and soon Josiah emerged. "Good morning," he said, running a hand over his face and then straightening his clothing.

"You are a good friend to help watch over our home," Mary said, hoping to keep away the threatening blush. "Thank you."

Josiah stifled a yawn, then nodded. "One ground is the same as another."

"Regardless, we are grateful," Martha said. She looked between the men. "We'd like to go to Simon the leper's house. Do you think it's safe?"

"Not without a guard," Josiah said immediately.

"He's right," Horeb said. "You might be stopped and questioned about the whereabouts of your brother. Some may not be kind."

"If Horeb wants to go with you, I will stay here and guard the house from those who want to pester the family of Lazarus."

"Josiah, you are so generous," Martha told him.

"Your family is important to me," Josiah replied simply.

Mary stepped toward his cart, which he had covered with a tarp. "I hope to see Jesus this morning at Simon's. Do you have any oils or precious ointments I could purchase from you?"

Josiah's brow crinkled as he joined her at the cart. He lifted a portion of the tarp, then sorted through some of the baskets. In a few moments, he produced an alabaster box. Carefully, he opened it to reveal a fragrant ointment.

Mary leaned in and inhaled. "It's lovely." And it smelled expensive, but she'd make the necessary sacrifices. "How much is it?"

Josiah shook his head. "It is a gift, all the way from Egypt."

Mary gaped at the merchant. "Surely I can't take this. I am willing to pay."

"I know you are," Josiah said, closing the lid to the box, then wrapping it in a cloth. "This is my gift to you and Jesus."

"You are very generous," Martha murmured, joining the pair at the cart.

Josiah handed over the wrapped box, then covered the goods in his cart.

"Are you ready?" Mary asked Martha.

The sisters linked arms, and with Horeb following a few paces behind, they wound their way through the back lanes toward Simon's house.

"Might we have a double wedding?" Martha whispered, keeping her voice low, for Horeb was not far behind.

"Hush," Mary said immediately. "I'm a fallen woman. You know that."

"I don't think Horeb cares much what others think." Martha waggled her brows. "What will you tell him when he asks?"

"He's not asking anything," Mary said, but it was too late. Her face had flushed hot.

Martha only smiled as they continued to walk. When they passed Tamara's home, the widow waved to them from her small garden plot.

Mary waved back but didn't stop to explain her errand.

Soon they arrived at Simon's home. As a blacksmith, he'd lost his living when he'd contracted leprosy the year before. A few in the village, including Martha and Leah, had left baskets of foodstuffs at his doorstep. Mary felt ashamed that she'd never reached out to or served the poor man. But she was learning, and she was growing.

Now that Simon had been cured of leprosy by Jesus, he'd received some recognition throughout the countryside, and he frequently had travelers stop at his home, bearing gifts and asking to hear his story in return.

Several men were in the front courtyard, speaking in lowered tones, and Mary recognized a couple of them as Apostles. Andrew and Simon Peter turned when she approached with her sister. She couldn't help but think of David's psalm about how Jesus would be betrayed by one of His followers. Mary nodded to the men, hoping that her neighborly status would allow her entry with no questions.

After all, she and Martha were no strangers to Simon. And Phebe and Eunice were inside somewhere, preparing food to feed Jesus and His Apostles.

Simon's door was open, and she could see others within, reclining or sitting on cushions. All men. And in their midst, there was Jesus. Mary's pulse leapt, and her emotions crashed about her—love for the Lord as well as deep sorrow for what must come.

Jesus was speaking about a nobleman, and Mary and Martha hovered in the doorway, not speaking a word as they listened. Mary recognized more of the Apostles, including Judas Iscariot and Thomas.

Jesus's words were gentle yet rang with firmness as He spoke. "A certain nobleman went into a far country to receive for himself a kingdom, and to return. And he called his ten servants, and delivered them ten pounds, and said unto them, Occupy till I come. But his citizens hated him, and sent a message after him, saying, We will not have this man to reign over us."

Mary met her sister's gaze as they listened, then her attention was drawn back to Jesus and His parable.

"When he was returned," Jesus continued, "having received the kingdom, then he commanded these servants to be called unto him, to whom he had given the money, that he might know how much every man had gained by trading."

Mary listened as Jesus explained that the first servant had invested his money and gained ten pounds. The nobleman was so pleased he gave his faithful servant authority over ten cities. The second servant had also invested and gained five pounds, and likewise, the second servant was granted authority over five cities. Jesus then told of the third servant. "And another came, saying, Lord, behold, here is thy pound, which I have kept laid up in a napkin: For I feared thee, because thou art an austere man: thou takest up that thou layedst not down, and reapest that thou didst not sow." Jesus explained that the nobleman then said, "Out of thine own mouth will I judge thee, thou wicked servant. Thou knewest that I was an austere man, taking up that I laid not down, and reaping that I did not sow."

"What does this mean?" Martha whispered.

Mary brought a finger to her lips to stall the answer as Jesus continued to speak of how, in the nobleman's absence, the first two servants had magnified their responsibilities, while the third servant hid his responsibilities away. Mary listened with growing interest as she connected the nobleman in the parable to Jesus Himself. He had been called King of the Jews and would soon be rejected by His own people.

"He is asking if we will serve Him or oppose Him," Mary whispered as they hovered outside the door. "Will we be like the first two servants who work diligently in His absence? Or will we go against His teachings when He is not here?"

Martha tightened her grasp on Mary's arm. "He is speaking of what will happen in Jerusalem?"

Mary nodded. "Let's go in now," she whispered.

But Martha tugged on Mary's arm before she could take one step inside. "I will go through the back to the cooking room to see what I can help with. I don't want to go through the large crowd."

Those within were starting to notice the two women at the door. A few of the men frowned, including Judas Iscariot. Others looked either curious or speculative. Simon saw her, but he was clearly as confused as the others. Surely he recognized them, though. An undertone of whispers reached Mary. *Who are they? What are they doing here?*

Mary's pulse shot up, but she knew that once Jesus left Bethany, she might never see Him again. "I'm going in," she whispered to Martha. "Come on."

But Martha pulled away from Mary's grasp. "If you must go, then go. I'll go around back."

So Mary clasped the alabaster box against her chest, and keeping her eyes lowered so she wouldn't have to meet the questioning stares of the men, she wove her way around the edges of the crowd, stepping over extended feet as the men asked questions about the nobleman parable.

She moved to Jesus's feet and bowed. His smile and greeting were tender when He called her by name. Then she presented the alabaster box and opened it. When Jesus nodded and extended His legs a little farther, she applied the oil to His feet and ankles, anointing them with the precious ointment. The action reminded her of when she had done this for her brother before his burial. Now Jesus . . . His death would come soon, and this was her act of anointing Him.

The men had quieted as she performed the anointing, and Simon asked, "Why must you go to the Passover feast in Jerusalem? You know that Caiaphas wants to arrest you."

Jesus's attention shifted to Simon. "Ye know that after two days is the feast of the Passover, and the Son of man [will be] betrayed to be crucified."

Simon nodded, and the men in the crowd shifted to hear better. Mary held her breath, her heart hammering at Jesus's words.

"Then will assemble together the chief priests, and the scribes, and the elders of the people unto the palace of the high priest, who is called Caiaphas, and will consult that they might take me by subtilty, and kill me."

Yes, Mary knew this, but she still ached at the words.

"But they will say," Jesus continued, "not on the feast day, lest there be an uproar among the people."

Mary's eyes burned with tears.

Martha entered the room just then, carrying a tray with food upon it. Eunice followed with another tray, then came Phebe with a wine jug to fill cups.

Mary had finished the anointing, and she felt like she couldn't breathe, couldn't absorb the Lord's words. She didn't want to start sobbing in front of the crowd of men. Her gaze met her sister's, and understanding connected them. Mary was ready to go, with or without Martha.

But Martha gave a nod of acknowledgment.

So Mary bade farewell to Jesus, sensing her farewell would be her last spoken words to Him, then she wove her way around the men until she reached the door. Martha was already waiting outside, and Mary grasped her arm.

"Are you all right?" Martha asked.

Mary blinked back the hot tears threatening to escape. "I don't think so. Let's go."

Martha didn't hesitate and said nothing else but simply hurried through the courtyard back to the lane. Horeb moved from the spot where he'd been waiting and followed them without a word. Horeb said nothing, but his guarding presence was comforting.

Once on the road for home, Mary took several deep breaths. "I anointed Jesus, and He knew it was in preparation for His burial." She swiped at her eyes with the edge of her mantle, soaking up her tears. "He prophesied, Martha, about His own Crucifixion."

"I heard a few of his words but not all," Martha said. "I am sorry, dear sister." Martha pulled her close, and it was all Mary could do to make it back home without completely falling apart.

CHAPTER TWENTY-ONE
Lazarus

"I AM TRYING TO STAY out of sight of any accusers and will return as soon as I'm able," Lazarus told his gathered family. Each beloved face was so dear to him that he hated to think he'd brought any angst upon them, either in his life or death.

"But where are you staying?" Leah asked.

"Not far from Zachary's tent," Lazarus said. The evening hour was late, but he hadn't dared return to his home when the sun was up. His disguise had been effective, and no one had stopped him as he'd hurried along the lanes. "Although I am relocating every day. Horeb is keeping the grove going."

He looked at Horeb, who sat on the edge of the family circle. Lazarus felt that he owed this young man so much. Horeb had protected his family in a time of great need, and now he was also watching over the operations at the grove. And then there was Zachary, who'd spent time away from his flocks during this precarious season to watch over Lazarus's family. Right now, he was with his sheep.

"How long will this go on?" his wife asked, her words more strained now. He could see the worry in everyone's eyes—his sisters', his sons', and even little Naomi's.

"Until Caiaphas doesn't feel threatened by Jesus's miracles and growing number of followers."

"You mean when Jesus is out of the way," Mary said in a near whisper.

Lazarus couldn't hide the truth from any of his family no matter their age or level of understanding. It was true. Tomorrow Jesus would enter the streets of Jerusalem. Lazarus had no doubt Jesus would be celebrated and the Jews of the city would rejoice at his arrival. But every hour was counting down until a trial and conviction.

"Our Lord will bring to pass a reconciliation with God so that we all might have eternal life and not die in our sins." Even though the words should have brought joy and comfort, right now, Lazarus's heart ached with a fierce pain knowing that Jesus had descended from on high and lived among sinners and would now sacrifice His own life on their behalf.

"We will go watch His entry," Mary said, grasping for Martha's hand.

Lazarus studied his two sisters. Jerusalem would be packed with visitors, those who were there for Passover. And Jesus had prophesied that Caiaphas wouldn't act yet, not when the city was full of His followers. Plus, the walk to Jerusalem was over a mile.

"Can we go with Mary too, Father?" Nathaniel asked, his young voice full of eagerness.

Lazarus looked at his wife. Her forty days of purification were not completed, and until she was considered ritually clean, she couldn't go out in public.

"I can watch over them," Horeb said.

Lazarus nodded. He wanted to go too but needed to be in disguise and not be associated with his family. "All right. I will go too, but we can't travel close together." So the plans were made.

Once Lazarus reached his makeshift tent that night, Zachary came over to check on him. Lazarus hadn't dared to build a fire for fear of attracting attention, but Zachary had shared a warm meal more than once.

The moonlight hovered above them as they spoke near the tent entrance. "You were able to see your family tonight?" Zachary asked.

"Yes, praise heaven."

"They are well, then? Your sisters?"

"They are well," Lazarus said. "I heard about Mary anointing Jesus."

"Yes, I heard as well," Zachary said in a thoughtful tone. "I spoke to Simon, and after Mary left his house, some of the Apostles complained that the precious ointment had been a waste."

Lazarus frowned. "Did Simon tell you what Jesus said?"

Zachary nodded. "Yes. Jesus said, 'Why trouble ye the woman? for she hath wrought a good work upon me. For ye have the poor always with you; but me ye have not always. For in that she hath poured this ointment on my body, she did it for my burial.'"

Lazarus drew in a breath. "He knows the end is near."

"You're right," Zachary said. "Jesus has declared it more than once. He told those in Simon's house, 'Wheresoever this gospel shall be preached in the whole world, there shall also this, that this woman hath done, be told for a memorial of her.'"

Lazarus stared at Zachary. "Jesus said that about Mary?"

"Yes." Zachary rested a hand on Lazarus's shoulder. "Your sisters are remarkable women."

"They are already grieving over Jesus," Lazarus said. "They want to travel to Jerusalem tomorrow. Horeb will offer protection."

"I will take Claudia as well," Zachary said. "I don't want her to miss something she will never forget her whole life, even if she doesn't fully understand. Perhaps I can keep an eye out for them."

"Thank you, Zachary," Lazarus said. "You have been so generous to my family over and over."

"I care for them," Zachary said simply. "They served my family when I had no one else to turn to when Claudia was so ill."

Lazarus drew his outer robe closer as the night's chill increased.

"There is something I need to ask you," Zachary said. "I plan to build a house this summer, and I'll be able to provide for a wife and future family. If I can have your blessing, I'd like to ask for Martha's hand in marriage."

Lazarus felt a smile grow. The idea had crossed his mind more than once, but he hadn't realized the full development of it.

"If my sister is in favor, then I give you my blessing."

Zachary smiled. "Thank you, my friend."

"And brother?"

With a laugh, Zachary said, "And brother."

After Zachary left, Lazarus settled in for the night, thinking about all that had happened since the day he met Horeb just outside of Galilee. At the time, he never could have comprehended the future events, and it was astounding to think of how his life had changed. He must have eventually drifted off to sleep because he was awakened by the melodic chatter of birds and the distant bleating of lambs.

Lazarus sat up, immediately alert. Had lambs been born in Zachary's flocks last night? After a quick meal of the honey cake his wife had given him last night, Lazarus began the trek to Zachary's flock. His sandaled feet quickly grew wet with the dew upon the spring grass, but he didn't mind.

He found Zachary kneeling next to an exhausted ewe who'd recently given birth. The infant lamb was already testing out its stamina on wobbly legs.

Zachary smiled as Lazarus joined him. Lazarus cleaned up the lamb with water from a goatskin and a dry swatch of fabric, then Zachary took over caring for the ewe. They worked in silence as dawn spread across the sky, turning the land golden.

Lazarus marveled at the new life that had been brought forth and the warmth and peace that filled him as a result. The miracle of birth echoed the miracles that Jesus had brought to the land, and now His sacrifice would become the greatest miracle of all.

"Can you feel that?" Zachary asked, looking at Lazarus. "The quiet, the peace?"

"Yes." Lazarus scanned the golden horizon. The spring breeze had warmed and carried with it the fragrance of wildflowers and new grass. "It's as if Adonai is telling us that everything will be all right."

Zachary nodded. "His guiding hand is in everything. These events are supposed to happen."

Lazarus exhaled.

"Do you want to use my staff," Zachary said, "to add to your disguise? No one will be looking for a shepherd or a man who needs support walking."

"True," Lazarus said. So he took Zachary up on the offer.

When the morning was still young, Lazarus traveled to Jerusalem. The roads were filled with others moving in the same direction. Up ahead, Lazarus kept track of his sisters and his two sons, as well as Horeb.

The crowds amassed at the city gate, and Lazarus was jostled more than once as he found a place to wait and watch. He heard the crowd's cheers before he saw Jesus's entrance through the gate.

Jesus rode upon a donkey, and those walking alongside him waved palm branches. Jesus's linen robes looked newly washed, and he sat strong and sure upon the donkey.

Lazarus's heart thundered as the crowds shouted Hosanna in praise of Jesus. Lazarus couldn't help but join in the crowds' praising. "Hosanna; Blessed is he that cometh in the name of the Lord: Blessed be the kingdom of our father David, that cometh in the name of the Lord: Hosanna in the highest."

The words echoed around him, and as Jesus grew nearer, Lazarus scooted farther back into the crowd. Even though he was among Jesus's followers, Lazarus didn't want to be recognized and mobbed. Word would get to the chief priests soon enough. In fact, Lazarus was sure there were some in disguise among the celebrants.

He watched as some in the crowd laid their robes in front of the donkey so that it had a clean path to tread upon. Jesus looked Lazarus's way, and their gazes connected for a long moment. When Jesus gave an imperceptible nod, Lazarus found his heart both filled and broken.

There were rumblings on the outskirts of the crowd, and Lazarus looked past the devoted followers. He'd never met Caiaphas, but by his priestly robes, Lazarus knew it was the high priest. Every fiber of Lazarus's being wanted to confront Caiaphas and explain who Jesus truly was; He wasn't a threat to the Roman governor. Jesus was the Prince of Peace.

Lazarus continued moving with the crowd after he saw Horeb walk with his sisters and Nathaniel and Rhode out of the city on their way back to Bethany. The crowds surrounded Jesus, continuing their praises.

"You came," someone said close to his ear.

Lazarus turned to see Simon from his village. "How did you know?"

Simon only smiled. "I saw you across the way. You'd best be careful."

"I thought I was," Lazarus said. "I wanted to see Jesus enter the city."

"He and His Apostles will stay the night in Bethany once again."

"You have been generous in your hospitality."

Simon clapped Lazarus on the shoulder. "I know you would do the same if you could."

It was true, but his own notoriety prevented that, and he didn't have a group of apostles offering protection.

As Lazarus traveled back to Bethany, he detoured through some fields and went into the rear courtyard of his house. He found Leah in the cooking room.

"Lazarus, you've returned," she said, rising to embrace him.

He pulled her close, then bent to kiss the top of the babe's head.

"Are you supposed to be working so hard?" he asked, smiling down at his wife. He missed being home and close to his family.

"I'm preparing the evening meal for when everyone returns." Leah pulled back, then handed the child to him.

He cradled the babe in his arms. "Do you think it's time we choose his name?"

Leah raised her brows. "I do."

Lazarus chuckled. "We talked about Asher, after your father, if we should have another son."

His wife's smile was soft. "Asher it is." She grasped his hand. "Thank you, husband. Now, tell me how long you can stay."

"For only a few moments," he said. "Where is Naomi? I should see her too."

"She's napping," Leah said. "Come on. You can peek in."

Lazarus followed his wife through the gathering room and along the corridor. They paused in the doorway of their bedchamber to see little Naomi sleeping in their bed. Lazarus crossed the room quietly, then sat next to his sleeping daughter. Her dark hair framed her face, and her lashes rested against her cheeks.

He softly ran a hand over her head without waking her. Then he bent over and kissed her forehead, breathing in her sweet scent.

Leah moved next to him and placed her hand on his back. "We miss you, husband."

Lazarus nodded. "I miss you too."

His wife wrapped her arm about his shoulder, and he slipped his arm about her waist, pulling her close.

He knew that in life, and in death, he never wanted to be separated from his family. And Jesus's sacrifice would make that possible.

CHAPTER TWENTY-TWO
Martha

MARTHA'S TEARS DRIPPED SLOWLY ONTO her cheeks as she stood over Yosef's grave site. She'd said goodbye to her husband three years ago, yet today, it felt different. Everything was changing. It felt like the whole world was changing. She'd agreed to marry Zachary, and she felt at peace about it.

But the tears continued to fall.

Her heart felt like it had cracked nearly in half.

Yesterday, Jesus, the Messiah, had been brought before Caiaphas and the Sanhedrin. Martha's tears burned hot as she thought about the news that Horeb and Lazarus had brought. They'd gone to Jerusalem to learn any news they could get.

What they'd heard was the chief priests, elders, and high priest had all testified against Jesus, and then the high priest had said, "Answerest thou nothing? what is it which these witness against thee?"

But when Jesus said nothing, the high priest continued. "I adjure thee by the living God, that thou tell us whether thou be the Christ, the Son of God."

Finally, Jesus answered, "Thou hast said: nevertheless I say unto you, Hereafter shall ye see the Son of man sitting on the right hand of power, and coming in the clouds of heaven."

Martha's tears might never dry. What happened next was hard to think about. Lazarus had told her that the high priest had rent his clothes, then accused Jesus of blasphemy. And the chief priests agreed that Jesus was guilty and should be put to death. Then, His accusers spat in His face and buffeted Him. Others smote Him with the palms of their hands and demanded that Jesus prophesy who had hit Him.

Martha sank to her knees and clasped her hands together as she prayed for Jesus and what He would face this morning. Lazarus had told her that He'd go before Pilate and Herod. What were the chances that Pilate would exonerate Jesus?

"None," Martha said to herself.

As the sun's rays rose above the horizon, there was no sound across the burial site above Bethany. It was as if the wind had stilled and the flowers didn't dare move.

Martha lowered her head, keeping her eyes closed as her mouth moved in a silent prayer. She didn't know how long she prayed. Time no longer mattered to her. Her knees ached where she'd been kneeling against the stony ground, but she didn't mind the pain. No, it was nothing.

"Martha," someone called.

She opened her eyes but saw no one. Who had spoken her name? Turning her head, she looked in the direction of the village and saw a woman hurrying toward her. Martha squinted against the morning's rays. It was past midmorning now, and the sky was bluer than the rivers and streams. Bluer than the swallows.

The woman grew closer, and Martha rose to her feet. "Mary!"

Mary didn't reply but began to run.

"What is it?" Martha asked as her sister reached her.

Mary's dark eyes were wide and her hair wild beneath her hastily donned mantle. "Josiah has brought word," she said in a breathless tone. "Jesus has been sentenced to death."

Martha had already known it would happen, but hearing the confirming words made her legs feel like water. "When?" she whispered.

"This morning." Mary reached for Martha's hands and squeezed.

The sun had nearly reached its zenith, and Martha realized that meant Jesus might have already met His death by now.

"Josiah saw Him nailed to the cross," Mary said in a quiet voice. "Then he couldn't bear to watch anymore and left, distraught. And he found me sitting on the stone wall by the fields."

"Is Lazarus still in Jerusalem?" Martha asked.

Mary nodded. "We should tell Leah about Jesus. She doesn't know."

"You're right," Martha said. The two sisters linked arms and headed down the hill toward their home.

As they did, the sky darkened, and Martha looked up. The previous blue was now marred by dark clouds billowing against the brightness of the day. "A storm is coming," she said in a faint voice; she'd never seen a storm move in so fast.

The sky was getting darker by the moment, but it wasn't rainy or windy.

Mary tightened her grasp on Martha as they neared their home. With the dark clouds hovering close to the earth, they'd hurried their step to get home quickly. The air was absolutely still. No wind. No sound.

"What's happening?" Martha asked as she reached out for the gate and opened it.

"The earth mourns," Mary whispered. "The very earth mourns."

Goose pimples raced along Martha's skin, and then she heard it. The quiet stillness was broken by the sound of a babe crying. *Asher.*

Martha turned the latch to their house and called for Leah.

"We're in here," Leah said.

The interior of the house was dim, and Martha followed the faint glow of an oil lamp coming from the bedchamber.

Before they reached the bedchamber, Martha heard a low rumbling coming from beneath the floor.

"What's that sound?" Mary said, her voice rising in pitch.

The rumbling moved into the wall, and then something clattered in the cooking room. Together, the sisters hurried to the bedchamber to find Leah with her children huddled on the bed, their eyes wide with fright.

"It is the Crucifixion, is it not?" Leah whispered.

"Yes," Mary answered. "The earth is rending her garments."

The earth noises had faded, only to be replaced by silence again. The dimness remained, cut only by the single oil lamp burning in the room.

Martha perched on the edge of the bed, watching the small family huddle together. She worried about her brother, about Zachary, but mostly she ached for what Jesus must be going through. In some of the worst cases, those crucified could hang on their crosses for days until dehydration and asphyxiation took them. Would this happen to Jesus?

"His body will need to be prepared for burial," Mary said in the quiet. "Josiah said Mary Magdalene and Mary, mother of James, were at the Crucifixion. They may need help."

Martha gazed at her sister, understanding immediately where she was going with this. "The darkness has not lifted."

"We can take our oil lamps."

"I will go with you," Rhode said, straightening from the bed.

A knock sounded from the back door of the house, and everyone stilled. Then Martha rose, her pulse jumping. "I will see who it is." Surely no one was hunting for their brother any longer, and their brother wouldn't be knocking on the door. Perhaps it was Josiah with more news.

She lit another oil lamp, then carried it through the house. A few things had fallen in the cooking room that she could straighten up later. Opening the back door, she saw Zachary standing there with Claudia clinging to his hand.

"Come in," Martha said immediately. "Are you all right?"

Zachary stepped past her, and Martha's heart rate immediately quickened at being so near to him.

"We came to check on you," Zachary said, his deep tones washing over her.

"Did you feel the earthquake?" Claudia asked in a trembling voice.

"I did." Martha pulled the little girl close, and she came willingly into her arms. Over Claudia's head, Martha's gaze connected with Zachary's.

His smile was soft, and it sent another flutter through her heart. With all that had happened this week, there had been no opportunity to communicate except through Lazarus: him telling her about Zachary's offer and then telling Zachary that she'd accepted.

"Do you want to see Naomi?" Martha said to Claudia, steering the young girl through the cooking room. Martha glanced over her shoulder and nodded at Zachary to follow them.

His footsteps followed, and Martha felt the shift in the air at his very presence. He didn't walk into the bedchamber. Instead, he waited in the gathering room while Martha took Claudia inside.

The two young girls immediately teamed up, and Mary's eyes brightened. "Maybe Zachary can accompany us to Jerusalem too."

The entire family knew about the agreed betrothal, of course, and if Rhode was going to be with them as well, perhaps it would be all right to have Zachary in their company; propriety wouldn't be breached.

"I will ask him," Martha said.

"I will go." Zachary's deep rumbling voice came from someplace down the corridor.

Both Mary and Leah smiled at Martha.

"And Claudia can stay with Naomi," Mary pronounced, loud enough for Zachary to hear from his location.

"Very well," Zachary said.

Now Martha's lips curved upward. "I will gather the oils and sweet spices in case we are needed to help."

When Martha had gathered what she needed and arranged it all in a bag, she and Mary set off toward Jerusalem accompanied by Rhode and Zachary. The dark clouds had finally shifted to allow the sun's rays through once again, and the early afternoon had grown warm.

As they walked, Mary sniffled, and Martha blinked back hot tears. It seemed the usual bustle of the road to Jerusalem was quiet. The travelers they encountered only nodded, and no verbal greetings were exchanged. Anytime she glanced at Zachary, he seemed to be feeling what she was: loss and grief over the Crucifixion of Jesus.

They were nearly to the city gate, and Martha slowed as they entered. A hush seemed to have fallen over the city. Beggars didn't line the road like usual, and street sellers had all disappeared for the beginning of Sabbath.

Mary paused by a group of women who stood together, one of them holding a babe.

"Any news of Jesus?"

The women turned and eyed Mary and their little party. One of the older women wearing a dark-blue mantle said, "Joseph of Arimathea has asked for His body. They are taking Him to Joseph's tomb, which he had hewn out in the rock on the west side of the Mount of Olives."

Martha tried not to react with shock. His *body*? "So He has died, then. Already?" she couldn't help but ask.

The woman nodded, distress clear in her face. "When it was still dark in the ninth hour, Jesus cried out, 'Eli, Eli, lama sabachthani?'"

"My God, my God, why hast thou forsaken me?" Mary whispered.

"They gave him vinegar to drink when He was thirsty," the woman continued. "And when the soldiers challenged Elias to come and save Him, Jesus said, 'Father, into thy hands I commend my spirit.' Then He died."

Martha wiped at her eyes. It seemed that Jesus had power over His own life, which only made His sacrifice all the more painful. He was innocent, and the Master of the world, yet He'd been treated horrifically.

"Let's go to the sepulchre," Mary said.

Martha turned to Mary. They'd come too far. Jesus had been buried closer to Bethany, on the Mount of Olives. Beside them, Zachary nodded, although his eyes were sad. "Yes, let's go," Martha told her companions.

The sisters made their way to the tomb site, passing along the quiet streets. As they crossed one of the alleyways, there were people kneeling upon the paved stones.

"What are they doing?" Rhode asked.

"I don't know," Martha said. The people looked like they were praying, and some of them were crying.

A young man who was kneeling nearby lifted his tear-stained face. "This is the road that Jesus traveled while carrying His cross beam to Golgotha."

Martha paused and looked from one end of the road to the other. "He carried His own cross beam?" The weight of the cross was too heavy for a single man to bear.

But the young man nodded, tears renewing. "The soldiers of the governor took Jesus into the common hall. There, they stripped Him and put upon Him a scarlet robe."

Martha glanced at Mary, who had tucked Rhode under her arm. Others on the road came nearer to hear the young man speak.

"They placed a crown of thorns upon His head." The young man wiped his face with his sleeve. "Then they put a reed in His right hand and mocked Him by kneeling down and saying, 'Hail, King of the Jews.'"

Martha's stomach clenched as dread pulsed through her.

The young man looked from Martha to Mary, then to Zachary. "They spit upon Him and took the reed. Then they smote Him on the head." He closed his eyes for a brief moment, then opened them again. "After they had mocked Him, they took the scarlet robe off and replaced it with His own raiment."

Martha reached for Mary's hand. Tears flowed down her cheeks.

"They took Him through the streets, and when He could no longer carry the cross, the soldiers pulled me from the crowd to carry it for Him." The young man held up his hands, which were scratched and bruised. "I wish I could have taken His pain away too."

Martha covered her mouth.

"What is your name?" Zachary asked quietly.

"Simon," the young man said. "I came from Cyrene to celebrate the Passover."

More people crowded around to hear his story, and he continued. "After they hung Him on the cross, they posted a sign over His head that read, 'This is Jesus the King of the Jews.'" Simon shook his head sadly. "Two others were hung on either side of Him, two thieves. The soldiers and chief priests kept on mocking Jesus. When they saw He was dead, a soldier pierced His side with a spear."

The people pressed around Mary and Martha, listening to Simon's retelling. As he began to repeat what he'd already told them, Martha tugged Mary's hand. She wanted to get to the sepulchre. She wanted to pay her respects at the burial site of Jesus.

No one in their party spoke as they walked, not even Rhode. When they reached the base of the Mount of Olives, the crowds grew thicker. The people were silently grieving as they sat among the rocks and wildflowers. It seemed that everyone had bruised hearts and minds.

Martha had never met Mary Magdalene or Mary, the mother of the Apostle James, but she was sure the two women near the tomb opening were them. They wore mantles covering their hair and stood close together as if offering each other support.

The sepulchre was covered with a large rolling rock so that the tomb was completely sealed up.

Mourners kept to themselves, quietly watching over the tomb. At a distance, the Apostles clustered in groups, and Martha noticed that one was not among them: Judas Iscariot. Where was he? The sun was sinking toward the western horizon, casting a deep orange over the pale rock of the tomb, making the color brilliant.

Martha sat with Mary and Rhode on a patch of grass. Zachary perched on a rock not far from them. Their small group was sober, and even Rhode kept still, his young expression revealing he was deep in thought.

"He will rise again," Mary said in a voice barely above a whisper. "King David said, 'For thou wilt not leave my soul in hell; neither wilt thou suffer thine Holy One to see corruption.'"

"I remember that psalm," Rhode said. "Later, King David said, 'O Lord, thou hast brought up my soul from the grave: thou hast kept me alive, that I should not go down to the pit.'"

"Yes," Mary said and reached for Rhode's hand.

But he stood instead. "Father?"

Martha turned to see Lazarus striding toward them, his face a mixture of relief and pain. "You are here. I have been looking for you all." He pulled his son into his embrace, then bent to kiss the cheeks of his sisters. Next he greeted Zachary. "Thank you for watching over my sisters."

Zachary nodded. "Always."

Lazarus settled among his family members. The group didn't speak for a moment, then Lazarus said, "You brought your spices."

Martha nodded. "The other women might need help, although the Sabbath is quickly approaching."

"I will introduce you," Lazarus said. He crossed to Mary Magdalene and Mary, mother of James, and spoke to them, then motioned toward his sisters.

Martha and Mary were already on their feet, and they joined their brother.

Mary Magdalene's smile was serene, but behind her dark eyes was the heartache all of them were feeling. "Thank you for bringing spices," she said in a quiet voice. "But the stone has been put into place to prevent grave robbing, and since the Sabbath approaches, we will not be able to administer the spices until tomorrow night or Sunday morning."

"Will you stay here, or do you need a place to rest your heads?" Martha asked. "You are welcome to stay at our home in Bethany."

The mother of James rested a hand on Martha's arm. "Thank you for your offer," she said. "We have a place to stay. But James had spoken with gratitude of the hospitality of the house of Lazarus. We are grateful for your service."

"And we are grateful for your sacrifice," Martha said.

After they'd spoken to the two Marys, Martha and her sister rejoined Rhode and Zachary in their vigil. The sun would completely set two hours hence, marking the beginning of the Sabbath day. They needed to be home by then, but for a few moments at least, they could sit in front of the tomb of Jesus and reflect on His teachings imparted both in life and death.

CHAPTER TWENTY-THREE
Mary

MARY DRESSED IN HER BEST clothing, donning the mantle she'd originally embroidered for her wedding to Isaac. That was all in the past now. She was still young, and she might marry someday, but it would be to an honorable man, a man who revered the Lord and lived his days in goodness.

She couldn't deny the many times her thoughts turned to Horeb, and it seemed that he watched her as well. His comment about wanting to be more than a business partner to her brother still clung to her mind. There had been no chance to speak more of it, though.

"Are you ready?" Martha said, cracking the door open to Mary's bedchamber.

Yes, Mary was ready, and it was a rare moment that her sister had to remind her of things that were important. Dawn had just barely graced the sky, but by the time they reached the other side of the Mount of Olives where Jesus was buried, the morning would be bright.

"Coming," Mary said, turning to see her sister's gentle expression of wariness. It was no wonder. Mary had spent most of yesterday crying, but today, she felt stronger, cleansed somehow. Her grief was but a small moment in the plan that the Lord had for the salvation of the entire world.

And today was the third day. Would He rise today the same way her brother had? Would she see Him?

Mary joined Martha at the door, and the two of them went downstairs. Martha had already prepared a meal for those in the household, although they were still sleeping.

Only Lazarus met them in the gathering room. "Ready?" he said with a smile.

Mary nodded, then walked out the front door with her brother and sister. Horeb would be joining them, and this sent a flutter through Mary's heart. Horeb was one of those good men, a man she could see a future with. But she wouldn't think of herself today. No, today would be about ministering to Jesus.

Prepared as always, Martha had brought along spices and food. She was ready for any necessity.

Horeb was already waiting by the village wall, and he straightened as they approached. After a simple greeting to her family, he smiled at Mary. Despite all the emotions that had been crashing through her for days, she smiled back. But with Horeb, there was no use hiding any of her thoughts. He moved to her side. "You are well?"

"I am better," she said with a hitch in her voice. She didn't know what Lazarus had told him, but she didn't mind that he was privy to her more personal part of life.

"I feel I have been tortured," Horeb said.

Mary looked at him in surprise. "What do you mean?"

"I don't know whether to weep for the mocking and abuse that Jesus went through at the hands of His own people or to rejoice that He has redeemed all men and women and provided a way to eternal life."

Mary exhaled. "I know what you mean." Tears burned in her eyes, but they were not ones she was ashamed of or ones she needed to hide.

"I do know that I am grateful to you and your family above all else," Horeb said. "If it weren't for Lazarus—"

"I know," Mary said with a quiet laugh. "I have heard this story many times."

Horeb chuckled. "So you have, but I will never stop telling it."

Her smile widened, and her pulse leapt all over the place. "I have no doubt."

Horeb's warm, brown eyes connected with hers, and in them, she saw the love he had for her brother, the love he often professed. But she also saw something else: a love that extended beyond Lazarus to *her*.

"Mary . . ." Horeb said in a quiet tone. "I hope you know how much I esteem you. Yes, I came to Bethany because of your brother, but there are many more reasons than him to stay."

"You are a kind and gracious man, Horeb," Mary said. "Our family is fortunate to have you as such a good friend."

"I hope to be more." Horeb's face had grown somber, an unusual thing for him. "Perhaps now is not the time for this discussion, but I hope to be more than a friend to you. Someday. When you are ready."

Mary knew the warmth coursing through her body had nothing to do with the sun.

"There's Mary Magdalene," Martha said before Mary could come up with any sort of reply to Horeb.

Mary looked away from Horeb, and sure enough, Mary Magdalene was coming toward them. They'd nearly reached the tomb on the slope of the Mount of Olives.

Mary Magdalene's mantle was askew, revealing part of her dark hair, which gleamed in the morning light. And . . . she was nearly running.

Mary's breath caught. Had something happened? Was it . . . something to do with Jesus?

Before she could question anyone in the traveling party, Mary Magdalene cried out, "He is risen! Jesus has conquered the grave!"

Mary's legs felt weak, and she could barely comprehend the words, but her heart soared with the news.

Mary reached for Mary Magdalene's trembling hands and held on tight as she told of finding the stone rolled back earlier that morning when she showed up to the tomb.

"We asked ourselves, 'Who shall roll us away the stone from the door of the sepulchre?'" Mary Magdalene said. "We entered the sepulchre, expecting to find Jesus's body wrapped in linens, but instead, we saw two men standing there in shining white garments."

Mary frowned. "Who were they?"

"They were angels." She released a slow breath, looking among the family members. "One said, 'Be not affrighted: Ye seek Jesus of Nazareth, which was crucified: he is risen; he is not here: behold the place where they laid him.'"

Everyone stared at Mary Magdalene. Her voice was stronger when she continued. "He said to go our way and tell Jesus's disciples, including Peter, that Jesus will meet them in Galilee." She brought her hands to her heart. "As you can see, we were stunned. We ran from the sepulchre and found Simon Peter and John where they were staying. At first they didn't believe us." Tears formed in Mary Magdalene's eyes. "I testify to you that the Lord had risen. He is no longer in the tomb."

Mary pulled the woman into her arms and held her tight. "We believe you, my friend. The prophecies have been fulfilled, and the Lord has broken the shackles of death."

"That is not all," Mary Magdalene whispered. She lifted her head. "After Simon Peter and John left, I remained by the sepulchre and continued weeping. Two angels were still inside, one sitting at the head and one at the foot where Jesus had lain. The angels said, 'Woman, why weepest thou?' And I told them

I was weeping because they'd taken away my Lord and I didn't know where he'd been laid."

Mary watched Mary Magdalene carefully, marveling at the unfolding story.

"I turned away from the tomb then and saw another man," Mary Magdalene continued. "I did not recognize Him and thought He might be the gardener. He asked me, 'Woman, why weepest thou? whom seekest thou?'"

Her tears started again, and her voice shook as she said, "I told him that if he'd relocated the body of Jesus, I would take the body away. But then, He called me by name, 'Mary.' And I knew who He was." She paused, gaining stronger control over her voice. "It was Rabboni, our Master."

Martha gasped, and Mary reached for her sister to steady her.

"I was so stunned," Mary Magdalene continued, "that I reached for Him. He said, 'Touch me not; for I am not yet ascended to my Father: but go to my brethren, and say unto them, I ascend unto my Father, and your Father; and to my God, and your God.'"

Mary wiped at the tears dripping down her cheeks. "The resurrected Lord showed Himself to you, Mary Magdalene, and you have been His messenger."

She nodded. "I have delivered my news to the disciples, and now I have delivered it to you."

Lazarus stepped forward. "Where are the disciples now?"

Mary Magdalene met his earnest gaze. "They have assembled inside the city in an upper room behind closed doors, waiting for further instruction."

"Then we will join them," Lazarus said.

When the group arrived at the upper room with Mary Magdalene and Mary, mother of James, everyone turned to greet them. James rushed over to embrace his mother.

"Come in," he said, greeting Lazarus, Horeb, and Zachary as well.

The women found an area on one side of the room where they sat and visited for a while. Only ten of the twelve disciples were in the room. Judas Iscariot had died, and Thomas wasn't present. As the day wore on, Martha shared the food she'd brought, much to the gratitude of the disciples. Broiled fish, honeycomb, and bread were the only selections, but no one complained.

Mostly, Mary listened to the disciples as they spoke of the last week of Jesus's life and the parables He taught even knowing that the trial was coming. Both Horeb and Zachary asked questions. The disciples also asked after Leah and the new child. Lazarus beamed as he reported that all was well.

In the early evening, someone appeared inside the room next to the door, and everyone went silent.

Simon was the first to speak. "Master," he said, falling to his knees.

Mary stared as Jesus walked into the room. Was He an angel? A spirit?

Jesus took a few steps into the room and stood in the midst of them. "Peace be unto you."

Mary gasped. His voice was the same. His eyes were the same.

The other disciples backed away as if they were afraid or uncertain.

"Why are ye troubled?" Jesus said, His voice resonating through the room. "And why do thoughts arise in your hearts? Behold my hands and my feet, that it is I myself: handle me, and see; for a spirit hath not flesh and bones, as ye see me have."

He wasn't a spirit, Mary realized, but a resurrected man, though not like her brother, Lazarus.

She looked at Horeb. He nodded, and they shared a look of wonder; he had understood the same thing she had. She took comfort in knowing that she was here with her family and Horeb and that they were all witnessing this together.

Jesus's gaze traveled the room as He extended His hands. The nail prints were dark with blood, and Mary looked down at His feet. Again the nail prints showed clear on His feet. And at His side, the spear wound was also visible.

The disciples sank to their knees before Him, marveling that He was alive again.

Jesus listened to the exclamations, then asked, "Have ye here any meat?"

Simon Peter smiled. "We have broiled fish and honeycomb."

Mary watched Jesus take the food and eat. He was real. He was not a spirit but a resurrected man of flesh.

After He'd eaten, He cast his gaze about the room again, taking in those who were there. "These are the words which I spake unto you, while I was yet with you, that all things must be fulfilled, which were written in the law of Moses, and in the prophets, and in the psalms, concerning me."

Mary nodded. She'd studied the laws, the prophets, and the psalms.

"Thus it is written," Jesus continued, "and thus it behoved Christ to suffer, and to rise from the dead the third day."

Mary felt Lazarus's gaze upon her, and she looked over at him. These were the very prophecies he'd taught her about. Martha linked arms with her, and the sisters sat close together, listening.

"And that repentance and remission of sins should be preached in his name among all nations, beginning at Jerusalem," Jesus said, His voice low but firm.

Mary leaned close to Martha. "Jesus wants the disciples to continue His work."

"Yes," Martha whispered.

Then Jesus motioned for everyone to gather closer. "Peace be unto you: as my Father hath sent me, even so send I you."

Mary felt goose pimples rise on her arms. Jesus was bestowing blessings upon the disciples to continue the work. She listened with rapt attention, wanting to remember every single word Jesus spoke throughout the night.

He had acknowledged the others in the room, but His words were mostly for His disciples. Mary became so engrossed in Jesus's teachings she hadn't even realized the entire night had passed and dawn had arrived. She should be tired. She should *feel* tired, but all she felt was awe and wonder.

When Jesus took His leave, His disciples followed.

Mary hung back with her family and Horeb and Zachary until the way was clear for them to travel back to Bethany without others questioning them. The experiences they'd had were too sacred to share right now.

"Jesus is asking His disciples to meet Him in Galilee," Lazarus said in a quiet voice.

"Will you go?" Mary asked her brother.

He scanned her face, and she didn't miss the hope in his eyes. Placing her hand on his arm, she said, "We will watch over Leah for you."

Lazarus nodded. "I know you will, and I appreciate the offer. I'll need to speak to her first."

"It has been a happy day," Mary said in a soft voice.

"Yes," Lazarus said, squeezing her hand. "Let's go home and share the news with Leah."

Martha joined them, and the sisters linked arms as they walked back to Bethany in the light of the morning sun.

Mary felt Horeb's gaze upon her more than once, but she didn't need to look at him to know that their hearts and minds were one.

So much had happened since meeting Jesus. So many miracles and beautiful words had been spoken. Mary knew that her life would never be the same.

The walk back to Jerusalem was filled with silent reflection on everyone's part. Mary could not believe the ways in which her life had changed over the past few months, both with her interactions with Jesus and with the arrival of Horeb.

Once back at their home, Lazarus and the others immediately went into the house to share the news with Leah. But Mary remained in the courtyard, reveling in the quiet of the approaching twilight for just a moment longer. The beauty of the violet and burgundy colors across the horizon made her heart full.

A shuffle of footsteps behind her caused her to turn around. Horeb was leaning against the wall, his focus upon her.

"I thought you turned off at the grove," she said. Horeb had said goodbye to them earlier.

The darkening sky made him a silhouette against the wall, but she could still see the warmth in his eyes—those eyes she'd become so fond of.

"I did turn off, and after checking on some things, I changed my mind about remaining there for the night." He straightened from the wall. "At least, I wanted to speak to you first."

"About what?" Mary asked in a light tone, although her pulse had begun to race as fast as a chariot.

"Mary . . ."

She drew her robe closer, although she wasn't in the least cold, as Horeb took a step toward her. She merely watched him, waiting, wondering if this was the moment . . .

"I have been crippled most of my life, but now that I've been made strong, I have hoped for things I'd never dared to before."

Mary tilted her head. "What are you hoping for, Horeb?"

Beyond them, the oil lamps glowed from inside the house, and above them, the moon and stars were creating their own light.

"I am hoping that someday I might be able to provide a home for a wife and family," Horeb said.

Mary couldn't help the desire to tease him. "I am sure you will."

"Mary . . ." Horeb shook his head with a smile. "I have never felt this way about another woman, and I never thought I would. But it would be my honor to take you to wife and provide for you the rest of my days."

They were the words that Mary had hoped to hear, though she hadn't admitted it to herself before. And on this day of all days. It was nearly too much, and her emotions surged.

"You're crying?" Horeb asked.

Mary wiped at the tears on her cheeks. "I suppose I am." Then she laughed. Horeb looked very, very confused.

"Oh, Horeb," she said. "I'd be honored to be your wife. But don't try to talk me into a double wedding with my sister, because I want my own."

Horeb's expression went through about four different variations. Then his face split into a grin. "You . . ."

Mary was suddenly pulled into his arms and pressed against his chest, confirming that his heart was beating as wildly as hers.

"Mary," he murmured. "Am I dreaming?"

"Not unless I am too," she whispered against his warm neck. This embrace was perhaps the nicest thing she'd ever experienced.

"Can I speak to your brother now?" Horeb said, pulling away and grasping her hands, his face so intent and so hopeful.

Mary laughed. "Yes, you may speak to him."

Horeb released her hands, then hurried toward the front door. There, he paused and looked back at her, his grin nearly brighter than the moon. "I still feel like I'm dreaming. What if I go inside and discover it has all been my imagination?"

Mary returned his smile. "Go, Horeb. I'll be here when you return. I promise."

CHAPTER TWENTY-FOUR
Martha

MARTHA DREW ON THE EMBROIDERED mantle over her loose hair. The mantle was the most beautiful piece of cloth she owned, made even more precious because Mary had made it. Over the past forty days, since the Resurrection of Jesus, so much had happened.

Her brother had joined the disciples and other followers as Jesus taught them in Galilee. Lazarus had returned home from time to time to report on Jesus's doings and teachings. Jesus had instructed His Apostles to return to Jerusalem, and even now, they might be passing by Bethany.

And last night, Lazarus had returned home for a very important event. For this morning, Martha would be married to Zachary. They had waited until Leah's days of purification had been completed so she could join in the festivities. And since it was the second marriage for both Martha and Zachary, they would have only a small wedding: family and a handful of friends, including Horeb.

Horeb, who'd taken over the business fully and rightfully, as he'd become their brother-in-law soon. Mary wasn't saying when their wedding would take place, but Martha was sure they wouldn't wait much longer.

Martha crossed to the window of her bedchamber and stood there for a few moments as she watched the sunrise shift from deep purple to magenta. Today would be a glorious day, and she was already smiling. She would be wed again, a wife again, and share her life again. She'd also have a daughter. Martha didn't bother to brush away the tears on her cheeks; there would be time for that in her preparations.

"She is awake, I tell you," a hushed voice came from outside her bedchamber.

Martha turned with a smile as Mary cracked open the door to peer in, Leah right behind her.

"Oh, good," Leah said. "You're awake. We have the bathing tub filled and the drapes set up."

"I told you she was awake," Mary said with a smirk. "And you can't wear that yet."

Martha slipped the mantle off. "I'm only trying it on."

"Very well," Mary said. "Come now, before the household awakes and catches you bathing."

Martha only smiled, then she draped the mantle across her bed so it wouldn't wrinkle. When she followed Leah and Mary to the cooking room, Martha found that her sister had indeed prepared a bath. She stepped through the drapes they'd hung. The water was scented, and as Martha slipped into the warm depths, she breathed in the luxury.

"This is wonderful. Thank you," Martha said. "Did you buy out Josiah's cart?"

From the other side of the curtain, both Leah and Mary laughed quietly. "Enjoy the bath," Leah said in an amused tone.

Martha was enjoying it, but she should still probably hurry.

"The oil in the painted vase is for your hair," Mary's voice said. "Do you need help?"

"I can manage." Martha wet her hair, then picked up the small vase and tipped it back. The scented oil was lovely, and Martha was still smiling as she ran the oil through her strands of hair.

She finished bathing quickly, and when she climbed out and pulled on her robe, the water was still warm.

"That was quick," Mary said as Martha parted the drapes and walked through. "You know you can be more indulgent on your wedding day."

"There is much to do still." Martha pulled a chair close to the cooking fire and sat down so that she could dry her hair against the heat of the flames.

Mary joined her at the fire and ran her fingers through Martha's damp hair, separating the dark tendrils so they'd dry faster.

"I'll plait your hair, and Leah will oil your hands and feet, then decorate them with henna."

Martha nodded, her eyes closing again as she allowed Mary's ministrations to relax her. Mary used a comb, making her sister's hair dry faster, then she also applied a few drops of oil to keep it supple.

As Leah knelt in front of Martha and began the intricate painting of henna on her hands, Mary plaited her hair. Later, when Martha dressed, she'd cover her hair, and the next person to see it would be her husband.

The thought sent a warm buzz through her. — me too!

"What are you smiling about?" Leah asked, curiosity in her tone.

"She's already dreaming about her wedding night."

Martha's eyes popped open. "I'm not dreaming."

Mary only laughed, and Leah grinned.

Martha was fairly sure her cheeks were flushed, but she was no young woman marrying for the first time. She and Zachary had both endured a lot of heartache and changes in life to once again find happiness in each other.

"You'll make a beautiful bride," Leah murmured as she began the henna process on Martha's feet. "Zachary will be very pleased."

Martha's cheeks went hot again. Her sister and sister-in-law wouldn't let her help with anything in the cooking room but insisted that she return to her bedchamber and get dressed.

"You have a morning wedding," Leah said, as if Martha needed reminding. "That means the guests will be here at any moment, so you can't be seen down here."

The word *guests* had been used liberally, Martha decided as she walked up the stairs to her floor. Once in her bedchamber, she drew out her best robe, the same one she'd worn on her first wedding day. Mary had added some more embellishments, though, and Martha was quite pleased with it.

Tonight, they would stay in Zachary's newly built home, and Claudia would stay with Mary and Leah, giving the married couple some privacy for a night or two.

Martha moved to the open window to take in the cool breeze that had begun. Below, in the courtyard, she saw people arriving. Her betrothed, in fact, with his daughter. As if Zachary sensed her watching, he paused in his step and glanced up at her window.

Martha drew back immediately but not before she caught his smile.

Zachary had been doing a lot of smiling as of late, and Martha supposed she had too, for they had much to smile about. Their wedding was not the only good news in their lives. Mary and Horeb would marry soon as well, on their own schedule.

And Martha was thrilled for her sister to have at last found an honorable man who would treat her gently and celebrate her love for learning and study. Horeb had been a blessing in all of their lives.

But now . . . Martha needed to go downstairs and join the wedding party.

"Martha," a young voice said outside her door. "We are ready."

Martha opened the door to find little Naomi standing there, her large brown eyes beautiful and her petite frame enclosed in a fine linen tunic. It seemed that Lazarus and Leah had spared no expense to dress her.

Warm scents of roasting meat wafted from the stairwell, and Martha knew she should be hungry, but her nerves had started to tighten.

"I'm coming," Martha said, but Naomi didn't move. "They want me to come down with you?"

Naomi nodded vigorously, and Martha smiled at that.

"All right." She turned into her room to pick up the mantle embroidered by her sister. She fastened it about her plaited hair until it was completely concealed. Then she added a veil that she'd wear during the marriage ceremony. Satisfied, she took Naomi's small hand, and the pair walked downstairs into the cooking room, where Lazarus waited for her.

"Ready, sister?"

"I'm ready," she whispered since her throat had grown tight. Her pulse was a steady thrum now.

Naomi ran ahead of them, and Lazarus led her through the back door. Martha knew that the marriage huppah had been set up in the back courtyard, but she hadn't seen it until now. She paused to take in the beautiful sight.

Leah and Mary must have gathered all the flowers in Bethany and intertwined them into the branches and leaves that decorated the huppah. Next, her gaze shifted to where Zachary stood beneath the huppah next to Elder Gideon.

Martha nodded to Elder Gideon, then studied Zachary. She'd never seen him so formally attired, and she wondered if it was all his own clothing from his earlier life in Jerusalem or if he'd borrowed some of it. His tunic was dyed a deep indigo and appeared to be of fine weave. His beard was trimmed short and his hair smoothed back and tied, topped by the groom's headpiece. The prayer shawl about his shoulders reminded Martha of the sacredness of what was about to happen.

Zachary smiled, and his entire face seemed to light up, only increasing the rate of her pulse. How had she been so blessed to have a second chance at marriage with a man who seemed devoted to her yet needed her as well?

Martha joined him beneath the marriage huppah, and Elder Gideon stood in front of them. Martha glanced at the other wedding guests—her nephews, Naomi, Claudia, Mary, Leah and her babe, Horeb, and Josiah . . . She cared deeply about every single person here.

Elder Gideon smiled at each of them, then recited the ceremonial words of the kiddushin.

Martha's pulse raced, and she felt warm all over. This was really happening.

"Zachary, will you take Martha as your wife according to the law of Moses?" Elder Gideon said.

Zachary's smile was confident. "Yes, I will."

Martha exhaled.

"Martha, sister of Lazarus," Elder Gideon said, turning to her now, "will you accept Zachary as your husband according to the law of Moses?"

Her heart could have easily burst at that moment. "Yes." She wanted to raise her veil and step into her new husband's arms.

Instead, Claudia stepped forward and handed over the cup of date-palm wine. Zachary thanked her and took a sip, then he handed the cup to Martha. She lifted her veil a little and sipped the wine. With a smile, she returned the cup to Claudia.

When Zachary produced a ceremonial ring, Martha wondered where he'd gotten such a precious piece of jewelry. She had told him to save his earnings for improving the house and to not spend it on her. But she really couldn't complain about her new husband's generosity. Zachary slid the ring on her finger and breathed out slowly.

"Behold, thou art consecrated unto me with this ring according to the law of Moses," Zachary said in a soft voice.

"From the beginning," Elder Gideon continued, "God created male and female."

Martha then moved to the next part of the ceremony. She walked around Zachary seven times, reflecting on how Joshua walked around Jericho seven times until the walls fell and how it took seven days to create the earth. Martha's emotions welled as she walked, then finally, she stopped in front of her husband.

Zachary's smile was tender as he moved close, then lifted her veil and placed the hem on his shoulder. His brown eyes sought hers, and in them, she only saw love as he moved the corners of his prayer shawl and placed them on her shoulder.

"What God hath joined together, let no man put asunder," Elder Gideon continued, a smile in his tone.

Leah and Mary stepped forward, holding garlands, placing one each atop of the bride and groom's heads. Claudia brought forward the bowl of blessed water, and both of them dipped their hands into the water.

"O Lord, please bless this union with the fruit of the vine," Elder Gideon prayed. "Bring them joy and sanctification. O Lord, our God, we humble ourselves in gratitude before Thee. O Creator of all things, we ask Thy blessing upon this husband and wife. We ask for the blessing of children born to this marriage. We ask Thee for the blessing of companionship and joy to be bestowed upon them. We praise Thy name, O Lord, our God. Amen."

"Amen," Zachary said, and Martha repeated it.

The other wedding guests each said amen in turn. Their voices rose in the quiet morning, as if on the rays of the rising sun.

Martha met Zachary's tender smile, and her pulse skittered as he drew her close with a sureness he hadn't displayed before. He leaned down, and Martha instinctively wound her arms about his neck. Zachary kissed her then, and she found she didn't mind in the least that her first kiss with this man was in front of her entire family. And his arms only tightened around her more.

Martha kept her eyes closed, blocking everything and everyone else out as she kissed him back. Only when those around them began to laugh and cheer did Zachary break off the kiss and lift his head. But he didn't release her. No, he grasped her hand, then they turned as one to receive congratulations from everyone.

She embraced her family members with one arm since Zachary still hadn't released her hand and seemed determined to keep them linked at all times. Martha embraced Leah last, who said, "You are a beautiful bride. Now, let's eat."

Martha drew away with a laugh, then they all reconvened in the gathering room, where Mary and Leah had superbly decorated the low tables. Zachary kept her hand tightly in his, and she felt rather amused by the whole situation. As they ate, Lazarus told them of the latest news of Jesus's ministry.

A knock on the front door made everyone pause. Had they forgotten to invite someone? Lazarus rose to answer the door, and a young man's voice could be heard by those at the tables.

"Andrew the Apostle sent me to bring you word," the young man said. "Jesus has appeared on the other side of the Mount of Olives to His Apostles and followers."

"Thank you for the message," Lazarus said. "You may tell Andrew that we have a wedding going on."

The young man took his leave, and Martha said, "We will all go."

All eyes turned on her.

"But it's your wedding day," Mary protested.

Martha looked up at Zachary to see if there was any objection in his eyes. When he smiled, she said, "A wedding day would be the perfect time to go."

Zachary squeezed her hand, and she wondered if he was ever going to let go.

The day was still early as the wedding party hurried through the streets of Bethany and out to the other side of the Mount of Olives.

Martha walked with Zachary hand in hand while Claudia held her other hand. The sun was warming the land and grass, and Martha's heart soared. She was surrounded by her family, and she had just increased it by two.

"How are you?" Zachary asked in a low tone.

She looked over at him to see his curved smile and lively brown eyes. He hadn't always had this aura of happiness and peace about him, and she was grateful she could see it now. "I'm well."

"Are you happy you became my wife today?" he asked, his tone amused, but he was eager for an answer.

"I am very happy I became your wife."

Zachary moved slightly closer and kissed her cheek.

"We are surrounded by people, Zachary," Martha said, although she was enjoying every bit of his touch.

He chuckled. "Yes, but I have a new bride, and I am happy if the world knows it."

She didn't mind if the world knew it, but it might be hours before they were alone, and she needed to keep a level head. "Are you happy you became my husband today?"

His expression grew serious at that. "More than you'll ever know, dear Martha."

She wanted to throw her arms about his neck, to embrace him, to kiss him, but she settled for tightening her hold on his hand.

Just then, they crested the hill and began to descend the other side. Below them the Apostles had gathered, all of whom Martha recognized and knew by name. Other followers were intermingled, along with some families with children. And in the midst of them stood Jesus, their resurrected Master.

Martha thought back to the first time she'd met Jesus and how she'd been so concerned with meal preparations and making a good impression on Him. His gentle words to both her and Mary had started a change in her heart, one of openness to new ideas and understanding that her spiritual development was more important than accomplishing her duties each day only to fall into bed exhausted and empty.

Lazarus led them to the outskirts of the circle of people, and Martha settled next to Zachary. He wrapped an arm about her shoulders, and she leaned into him. Claudia sat in front of them, keeping little Naomi next to her. The two girls sitting together, their gazes focused on Jesus as He spoke, created an image Martha would never forget.

Jesus was the Messiah, but He was also her brother. Like Lazarus, her brother of flesh and blood, Jesus cared for her well-being. His compassion extended beyond a single woman or a single family but reached to all mankind—Jew or Gentile. He was the new way.

"And, behold," Jesus said in His deep, resonating voice, "I send the promise of my Father upon you: but tarry ye in the city of Jerusalem, until ye be endued with power from on high."

"What is the power from on high?" Martha heard Nathaniel whisper.

Mary leaned toward him and said, "The Holy Ghost."

"For John truly baptized with water," Jesus said. "But ye shall be baptized with the Holy Ghost not many days hence."

Andrew stood from where he sat and asked, "Lord, wilt thou at this time restore again the kingdom to Israel?"

Jesus looked about the crowd, then answered, "It is not for you to know the times or the seasons, which the Father hath put in his own power. But ye shall receive power, after that the Holy Ghost is come upon you: and ye shall be witnesses unto me both in Jerusalem, and in all Judea, and in Samaria, and unto the uttermost part of the earth."

Martha's skin tingled at the words. Jesus wasn't only speaking to His Apostles but to all His followers. She felt it to her very bones as His gaze encompassed every single person in the gathering.

And then His expression shifted into a gentle, loving smile, and Martha could literally feel the love emanating from His countenance. If she hadn't been sitting with dozens of witnesses, she might have thought she'd dreamed the next events. Before her very eyes, Jesus rose from the ground, His feet with their nail prints still visible, leaving the earth.

Jesus spread His hands, but in no other way did His body move. He continued upward, toward heaven.

The crowd was absolutely silent, and Martha knew they were all struck with amazement.

Jesus was ascending to heaven.

The Messiah was returning to His Father.

Martha hadn't even realized she'd been crying until the tears dripped onto her clothing. Her chest hitched when little Naomi turned and asked her father, "Where did He go?"

Lazarus wiped at his own tears. "Jesus returned to heaven, but He will be back, dear Naomi. He will return again."

The west side of the Mount of Olives returned to its stunned silence, and only the occasional sniffle could be heard among the witnesses.

It was a long time before any of the Apostles stood, and Martha watched as several of them conversed with Lazarus, wondering and marveling at the ascension. The Apostles had been given instructions, and now it was time for them to begin their ministries.

Mary reached a hand toward Martha, and the two sisters embraced, still sitting on the ground. "I have no words," Martha whispered to her younger, wiser sister.

"I will help you find them," Mary said, tenderness in her voice.

When she drew away, Martha smiled through her tears as Zachary held out his hand to pull her to her feet. She rose, then fell into his arms. He pulled her close and kissed the top of her head. Martha had never felt so whole in her life. Reconciliation was real, and she would someday be reunited with her lost loved ones. But for now, she would rejoice in the love she'd found on earth, and she'd spend the rest of her days in service to her God.

Scripture References by Chapter in Order of Reference

Chapter Four
Matthew 6:33; Matthew 11:28; Luke 18:42; Mark 2:5; Luke 5:23; Matthew 8:2–3

Chapter Five
Micah 5:2

Chapter Seven
Isaiah 9:6; Isaiah 7:14; Micah 5:2

Chapter Eight
Micah 5:1; Isaiah 50:6; Isaiah 53:5

Chapter Nine
Matthew 18:4

Chapter Eleven
Luke 10:25–37

Chapter Thirteen
John 14:27; Matthew 17:20; Matthew 18:12–13; John 8:31–32; Matthew 19:16

Chapter Fifteen
John 11:3

Chapter Seventeen
John 11:21–23, 25–27, 32, 34, 36–37, 39

Chapter Eighteen
John 11:39–44, 54–55

Chapter Nineteen
Matthew 20:17–19; Zechariah 9:9; Isaiah 53:1, 3; Psalm 41:9; Psalm 55:12–13; Matthew 20:18–19

Chapter Twenty
Matthew 26:6–13; Luke 19:11–27; John 12:1–7; Matthew 26:2–5

Chapter Twenty-One
Matthew 26:8–13; Mark 11:9–10; Isaiah 9:6–7; Mark 11:11

Chapter Twenty-Two
Matthew 26:62–68; Matthew 27:57–60; Matthew 27:46, 48; Mark 15:36; Matthew 27:49; Luke 23:46; Matthew 27:27–32, 37–40; Psalm 16:10; Psalm 30:3

Chapter Twenty-Three
Mark 16:1–7; Luke 24:4; Mark 16:10–11; John 20:11–17; Luke 24:36, 38–39; John 20:20; Luke 24:41–42, 44, 46–47; John 20:21

Chapter Twenty-Four
Acts 1:4; Luke 24:49; Acts 1:5–8

ACKNOWLEDGMENTS

THE STORY OF MARY AND Martha and their brother Lazarus has always been a pinnacle event for me in the New Testament. With multiple sisters of my own, and now sisters-in-law, matters of the hearth and home are individual to each woman. I've often wondered who this small family in Bethany was and what it would have been like to have such a friendship with Jesus. When the time came to write this novel, author friends Rebecca Connolly and Jen Johnson and I had many discussions about the characters and relationships of these three siblings. I'm grateful for their insights and encouragement throughout the drafting process.

I'm also grateful to my parents, Kent and Gayle Brown, for their willingness to read the first draft and give valuable feedback. My father, S. Kent Brown, is a biblical scholar, and we had many discussions both before and during the creation process. One of the most significant things my father told me was when Jesus encouraged Mary to learn at his feet, this was a message to everyone—that the Savior supports the education of women.

This is the first book in many years on which I haven't worked with editor Samantha Millburn. She took on a manager position within the publishing company, and I'm grateful for her guiding light. Editor Ashley Gebert took on this manuscript and did an excellent job. Many thanks go to the many people who have a hand in this book's production, including Robby Nichols, Phil Reschke, Amy Parker, Margaret Weber, and their teams.

Finally, I'd like to thank my husband, Chris; my children, Kaelin, Kara, Dana, and Rose; and my father-in-law, Lester Moore. Their continued support is deeply appreciated.

About the Author

HEATHER B. MOORE IS A *USA Today* best-selling author of more than a dozen historical novels and thrillers written under the pen name H.B. Moore. She writes women's fiction, romance, and inspirational nonfiction under Heather B. Moore. This can all be confusing, so her kids just call her Mom. Heather attended Cairo American College in Egypt and the Anglican School of Jerusalem in Israel and earned a bachelor of science degree from Brigham Young University in Utah. Visit Heather's website here: www.hbmoore.com.